HIKER'S GUIDE
TO
GLACIER
NATIONAL PARK

HIKER'S GUIDE TO GLACIER NATIONAL PARK

ISBN 0-915030-24-1

Printed in the United States of America

Published by

GLACIER NATURAL HISTORY ASSOCIATION
West Glacier, Montana 59936

INTRODUCTION

Glacier National Park is not only one of the finest for viewing scenery and wildlife but also one of the most rewarding to hike. With its estimated 1120 kilometers of trails, it is undeniably a "hiker's park." Scenery this beautiful when viewed from the road can only be better when explored on foot. There are beaver ponds and green bog-orchids in the lowland valleys and meadows; there are cool, dark forests at the middle elevations; and the highcountry is a wind-scoured world of peaks and unsurpassed views.

The hikes we describe in this book cover a wealth of country, including all of the different types of areas. Some follow the Continental Divide; some climb to fire lookouts and alpine meadows; others wander through woods and along lakes and streams or crest in the high passes.

This is an exciting park to visit, and the best way to see it is from the trails. The wildlife seen along the roads and in the campgrounds is an interesting but tame version of what waits to be seen in the backcountry.

Among the more interesting birds to be seen while hiking are the harlequin duck, blue grouse, white-tailed ptarmigan, Clark's nutcracker, dipper, varied thrush and gray-crowned rosy finch. Many of these species of birds are very selective in their choice of habitat and will be seen only along certain trails.

In addition to the birdlife, Glacier teems with interesting mammals. Those of us who have done much hiking in other parts of the country may be used to a wildlife that has been harassed to the point of being elusive and scarce. Here the animals have been loved and protected for so long that many of them accept man almost too casually for their own good. There are two species of bears in the park--the grizzly and the black--and both should be admired only from a very respectful distance. Mountain goats, bighorn sheep, hoary marmots and Columbian ground squirrels are inclined to be quite tame. Other mammals such as the pika and the beaver may require some time and a little patience to see.

The wildflower display is lavish at times. We have seen entire slopes blanketed by beargrass in bloom, whole meadows of glacier-lilies, rocky screes accented by moss campion and alpine forget-me-nots. It is not unusual to see 25-100 species of wildflowers blooming along a single hike.

There are over a thousand species of vascular plants recorded for the park, and others will doubtless be discovered in the future. Among our favorites are the green bog-orchid, alpine mitrewort, meadow death-camas, moss campion, blue columbine, subalpine buttercup, queencup beadlily, shooting star, elephanthead, and butter and eggs toadflax. Obviously, Glacier's trails do not lend themselves to pellmell hiking; they invite (demand!) leisurely hiking and lots of looking.

The park is heavily forested below timberline; however, the number of individual species is not overwhelming. The most common trees are Engelmann spruce, Douglas fir, western red cedar, western larch, western hemlock, lodgepole pine and subalpine fir. Shrubs compensate for the short growing season by spreading riotously, sometimes crowding the trails and obscuring visibility.

Glacier Park is a textbook example of many geological phenomena. Its very name derives from the fact that its major valleys and many other features were carved by glaciers. There are some fifty glaciers still in the park, but these are of much more recent origin than those which created much of the park's basic landscape. The mountains are sedimentary rock, and evidence of their deposition in a prehistoric sea is common in rocks containing fossilized algae colonies, ripple marks and mudcracks. Many of the rock stratas have been tilted and uplifted by forces of incredible magnitude.

While many laymen find the study of geology a rather dry pastime, the geology of this particular park, like that of the Grand Canyon, is too striking to be ignored. We found that cause and effect were easily interpreted once we had a few basic facts to go on. We suggest you trail along on one of the naturalist-led hikes in order to acquire a basic knowledge of the park before attempting to interpret the natural history for yourself; it helped us considerably.

We try in this book to pass on as much information as space allows, but you will undoubtedly want to be fortified with as much information as possible. Insure an enjoyable trip by planning it carefully and using sound judgement so that no harm comes to you or to the park.

HOW TO USE THIS BOOK

All of the hikes and trails described in this book were carefully hiked, measured, mapped and described by us in 1977. While every effort was made to maintain accuracy and to highlight those points of most significance to a hiker making the trip for the first time, this book should still be considered only an aid. You must depend on the physical trail (or route), the landmarks, careful planning and common sense to get you safely from place to place in an area as large and complex as Glacier National Park. In general, the trail system is excellent and well maintained. We know of no other area with so large a trail system in such fine condition.

There may be occasional places along many of the trails where the route is obscure. Usually this is only for very short stretches where luxuriant growth of shrubs may have obscured what was a clear route earlier in the year. Mud and snow occasionally become more than a minor nuisance. We suggest that you commit your back-trail to memory; you might have to make a hasty retreat that way in case of an emergency. If, for some reason, you are not able to follow a trail, seriously consider returning to the trailhead. Don't risk becoming lost. All of the trails described in this book were in excellent condition when we hiked them, and there should be no problems. Still, be mentally prepared

so that an unexpected obstacle won't throw you into confusion.

On the subject of confusion, Glacier's peaks, trails, valleys and other features all look alike when you are in the park for the first time. The longer you are in the area, the more distinct the landmarks become. Topographic maps are particularly helpful for identifying landmarks--if the maps are used correctly. The various trails will eventually begin to "fit together" in your mind as well as in the field.

Know where you are at all times, and know exactly where you are headed. This is second nature to most hikers, but it may require a little effort for a novice to hiking--especially with so many pleasant distractions. If you plan an extensive hike, give your written itinerary to a park ranger.

Most of the trailheads and junctions are signed. Occasionally porcupines, bears, or thoughtless humans will damage or remove signs. The distances indicated by the signs are National Park Service figures and may vary slightly from some of the distances which we measured independently. In general, the two sets of figures are very close.

Within Glacier's extensive trail system are a number of trails which have not been maintained for years. Some of these are completely obliterated by time and vegetation while all or parts of others can be followed by experienced hikers prepared to spend the night out. We have hiked some of these overgrown "routes," and they really are more work than fun. Unless you have a specific destination, such as a peak, there is little reason to thrash about on the old trails or routes. Of the 1120 kilometers of maintained trails in the park, we have described 291 kilometers of what we feel are excellent hikes. There are 25 hikes described in this book, all of which we researched as one-day hikes. Many lend themselves to overnight trips, and several of the longer ones are probably too strenuous for the unconditioned hiker to undertake as a one-day outing. We have designated as "overnight" those hikes along which camping is permitted. Check at any ranger station for current status of camping areas. Keep in mind when planning your hike that a Backcountry Camping Permit is required if you plan to stay out overnight.

For the sake of brevity, we refer to Going-to-the-Sun Road as "Sun Road."

Many of the hikes described in this book can be started from the opposite direction. As a matter of practicality, we had to begin our description at one end or the other.

We have made no effort to rate the hikes as to degree of difficulty, such as "easy," "moderate" or "difficult." You will have to study the maps and information provided and decide for yourself whether or not you are in good enough condition and have enough time to make a particular hike. We do suggest that you acclimate yourself to Glacier's environment by starting out with short hikes and gradually building up to longer ones. All of the hikes described involve hiking in rugged country, and climbs and descents of some degree should be expected on all hikes. Pace yourself, and don't try to tackle too much at once. Rest often along the trail-- take in the scenery, and learn something of the plant and animal life. Hiking in Glacier should not be undertaken as though you were participating in an athletic event.

Always hike with at least one other person. Not only can the shared experience be enjoyable, but if you should come to a vague stretch of trail, one person can stay on the established trail while the other hikes ahead, looking for the route. A prearranged signal can be used to summon the waiting hiker if the trail is found ahead. If the trail cannot be found, the hike should be abandoned or re-done after getting additional information from park personnel.

Another advantage of having a hiking partner is that there will be someone who can go for help in case of emergency.

All hikers should consider carrying a whistle and working out with their hiking partners a prearranged method of whistle communication. A whistle can also be useful in an emergency should you be immobilized and need to attract help. It is more efficient than yelling and uses less energy.

How far you can hike in a single day in Glacier will depend on many factors, including your physical condition, the degree to which you are acclimatized to the environment (including the higher elevations), the weight you are carrying, the steepness of the terrain, the weather, and unforseen developments. The hiking pace will vary greatly from one person to another. We prefer to hike slowly in order to see as much as possible, pausing often to watch the wildlife or admire the view. If you're out for a dayhike, which is a great way to see much of Glacier, be sure to allow enough time to be back before dark. Don't be so intent on reaching a destination that you put yourself under much the same pressure as you faced in five-o'clock city traffic. Many people overestimate the speed at which they hike and the distance they can cover--and if you attempt to cover too much, you may be setting yourself up for trouble. Besides, hiking head-long through the park is going to diminish the quality of the experience.

Looking back, we've found that our fondest memories are a montage of small happenings and discoveries that took place against a backdrop of elegant scenery. Some of the little things that come to mind include a pitched battle between two colonies of ants along the Otokomi Lake Trail; pikas among the rocks along the Highline Trail; and Sharon's first encounters with forget-me-nots and mountain goats. While toiling up the Mount Brown Lookout trail, Sharon was heard to grumble that "there had better be something good on top." When she rounded the last bend and came face to face with her first mountain goats, the strenuous climb was not only justified but completely forgotten. Then there was the spruce grouse Dick was trying to photograph. He would just about have her in focus when she would run up to the camera and peck him. He got about twenty exposures of an aggressive spruce grouse stalking into the brush. We have smiled over that episode many times since returning home. So...try to capture the types of memories that will give you pleasure long after you've left the park.

MAPS AND DESCRIPTIONS

Maps are an important part of this book, but remember that they are only visual aids. They are no substitute for common sense and being prepared for the unexpected. The alignments of all trails in this book were carefully checked against the maps, but keep in mind that trail alignments are subject to change.

The maps in this book are reproduced from United States Geological Survey maps (usually referred to as topographic maps or "topos") except for a single line map used to show the locations of the topographic maps. These maps can convey a wealth of information, and an experienced map reader can easily learn a great deal about an area without actually going into the field.

We made only a few changes of trail alignments on the maps. These were usually associated with maintenance problems--relocation of a washed-out bridge, erosion problems resulting from floods, etc. The dashed lines used to indicate trails on the original topos are very light and difficult to see in the field, so we have used a darker dashed line to show the alignments of the trails we describe and have adjusted the alignments in those few places where we found it warranted.

We found it relatively easy to confirm trail alignments on the original maps if there were plenty of landmarks or if the area was open. In a few places, dense forest or an absence of distinct landmarks made it difficult to pinpoint our location on the map. Glacier's trail system remains very stable year after year, but keep in mind that trails may occasionally change. We didn't find changes to be a problem in researching this book; we mention it only as a possibility to be considered.

Most of the trails in Glacier National Park are so well defined that following them is a pleasure. Patches of snow or exuberant growth of shrubs may obscure short stretches of some trails, but usually it is just a minor nuisance. Glacier's trails are technically "open" unless officially closed by the superintendent, in which case the trailhead will be posted. However, we strongly recommend that you limit your hiking to those trails that park personnel have "worked." Trails may be open yet not recommended for travel due to a variety of reasons including untreaded snow, heavy windfalls, avalanche debris and high, flooded streams.

When researching and mapping a hike, we use the "prediction method." We study the map carefully, looking for significant contour lines and landmarks. We try to pinpoint our position on the map, then predict what the trail will do in the next hundred meters or so. Usually the trail does as predicted--crosses a creek, starts to climb steeply, drops down to a lake, etc. If it doesn't, we sit down and carefully determine why the map and the terrain don't match. Invariably it is because we weren't where we thought we were when we made our prediction. Topographic maps are excellent aids but require careful study and a lot of experience if they are to be used to best advantage.

Always know where you are, both in the field and on the map. There is always the possibility that you may have to pinpoint a certain location so that a rescue team can go directly to a spot where, for example, someone is injured or was last seen.

Most if not all of the hikes described here can be made without using a map, but the hike probably won't be as interesting. You may come to unexpected junctions or make a wrong turn or underestimate distances. For curiosity's sake as well as for safety's sake, we try to identify any obvious peaks, streams, lakes and other significant features along a trail.

We have made several changes on the topo maps in addition to darkening the trail dashes and re-aligning the trails in a few places. We have indicated every kilometer (1.0, 2.0, etc.) along the hike, starting our measurements from the trailhead. We used a measuring wheel to calculate our distances. In fact, we usually used one measuring wheel with two counters and a back-up wheel with a single counter. With two wheels and three counters, we feel relatively safe when we quote distances. The letters along the trails on the maps (A, B, etc.) refer to various features and points mentioned in the text. For example, "point C (4.1 km)" would refer to point C on the map, and the 4.1 indicates that point C is 4.1 kilometers from the trailhead.

Glacier National Park is covered in detail by a series of 41 topographic maps (7.5-minute), and there is a single, large topo which covers the entire park. The maps in the series are generally the most useful because they are more detailed. The large map is useful for planning longer hikes which involve a number of trails. It is also useful for identifying distant peaks from various locations. The following diagram shows the relationship of the 7.5-minute topo maps to each other.

These maps may be purchased from the United States Geological Survey or at park visitor centers.

All of the trails described in this book are overlaid on sections of these topo maps, so it is important that you become proficient at interpreting them. Many of the topo map sections have been reduced from their original size, although some of the sections are reproduced at actual size. The approximate scale for each of the various maps can be determined by studying the distance between kilometer marks along the trails.

1. The magnetic declination--an important figure for anyone using a compass--varies slightly with the area of the park involved, but the variation is only one half degree.

20°

TRAILCREEK 1966	KINTLA LAKE 1966	KINTLA PEAK 1968	MT CARTER 1968	PORCUPINE RIDGE 1968	MT CLEVELAND 1968	GABLE MTN 1968	CHIEF MTN 1968	PIKE LAKE 1968	GOOSE LAKE 1968	HALL COULEE 1968
WHALE BUTTES 1966	POLEBRIDGE 1966	QUARTZ RIDGE 1968	VULTURE PEAK 1968	MT GEDUHN 1968	AHERN PASS 1968	MANY GLACIER 1968	LAKE SHERBURNE 1968	BABB 1968	DUCK LAKE 1968	WETZEL 1968
MOOSE PEAK 1966	CYCLONE LAKE 1966	DEMERS RIDGE 1966	CAMAS RIDGE WEST 1966	CAMAS RIDGE EAST 1968	MT CANNON 1968	LOGAN PASS 1968	RISING SUN 1968	SAINT MARY 1968	FOX CREEK 1968	HORSE LAKE 1968
WERNER PK 1966	SKOOKOLEEL CREEK 1966	HUCKLEBERRY MTN 1966	MC GEE MEADOW 1966	LAKE MC DONALD WEST 1968	LAKE MC DONALD EAST 1968	MT JACKSON 1968	MT STIMSON 1968	CUT BANK PASS 1968	KIOWA 1968	STARR SCHOOL 1968
BEAVER LAKE 1962	WHITEFISH 1962	COLUMBIA FALLS NORTH 1962	HUNGRY HORSE 1962	WEST GLACIER 1964	NYACK 1964	STANTON LAKE 1964	ST NICHOLAS 1964	MT ROCKWELL 1968	SQUAW MTN 1968	EAST GLACIER PARK 1968
RHODES 1962	ROSE CROSSING 1962	COLUMBIA FALLS SOUTH 1962	DORIS MTN 1962	NYACK SW 1964	MOUNT GRANT 1964	PINNACLE 1964	ESSEX 1964	BLACKTAIL 1968	SUMMIT 1968	HYDE CREEK 1968
BLUE GRASS RIDGE 1962	KALISPELL 1962	CRESTON 1962	HASH MTN 1962	JEWEL BASIN 1964	PIONEER RIDGE 1964	FELIX PEAK 1958	NIMROD 1958	MT BRADLEY 1958	RED PLUME MTN 1958	CRESCENT CLIFF 1958

2. All map sections are reproduced in a north-south alignment.

3. The contour interval is the elevation change represented by the distance between contour lines. (These lines are brown on the U.S.G.S. maps but are easy to distinguish on the black and white maps in this book.) The contour interval, which is either 40 feet (12.2 meters) or 80 feet (24.4 meters), varies between maps.

We have made no attempt to describe every facet of every trail but have tried to describe those features that we considered to be of most importance or interest. No two hikers would describe a trail exactly the same way, and you could have difficulty where we had none, or you could encounter different conditions. The conditions of trails may vary from year to year and with the season. Where we had a dry trail, you might find yourself wallowing through mud. Except for a few patches of snow along a few hikes, all of the trails were snow free when we researched this book. In some other year, this might not be the case.

For each of the hike descriptions, we have included the following basic information as shown in this example from the Cracker Lake hike:

Length:
One way - 10.4 km
Round trip - 20.8 km
Dayhike or overnight
Season: Early July
Vehicle shuttle: No
Elevation extremes: 1475-1853 m
Topographic maps:
Many Glacier
Lake Sherburne
Logan Pass

An explanation of the above items follows.

Length: The length one way is the distance from the trailhead to the destination (10.4 kilometers in the example). Since it is necessary to return via the same route, the round-trip distance is also given (20.8 kilometers). If a hike makes a loop, only the round-trip distance is given. We have not listed a round-trip distance for hikes where it seemed more sensible to arrange transportation back to the trailhead.

Dayhike or overnight: Cracker Lake presently has a camping area (see ''Backcountry Regulations''), so this hike can be done as a dayhike or an overnight trip. If we list a hike as a dayhike only, it means that no camping is permitted along that particular hike. Check at a ranger station for current policy on each area.

Season: The opening of individual trails varies from one year to the next, depending on such factors as water or snow on the trail, damage to bridges, and scheduling of trail crews which go in early in the season to brush and repair. It is imperative that you ask a ranger for the list of trails that are already open for the season. The list will grow as the season and the trail crews progress. Many of the lowland trails open in June unless it is an unusual year. Several of the highcountry trails may not open until sometime in August. The average opening date for the Cracker Lake hike is early July, but remember that this is only a ballpark figure that will vary from year to year.

Vehicle shuttle: In the case of the Cracker Lake hike, it is necessary to return via the same route; therefore, no ride is needed back to the trailhead. A number of hikes start and end at a road, with considerable distance in between. For those hikes, it makes better sense to arrange transportation back to the trailhead, assuming your vehicle is parked there. Better yet, someone may be able to drop you off and pick you up at the other end. If a vehicle shuttle is indicated, be sure to allow extra time if you must hitch a ride back to your car. (Some hikers prefer to leave their car at the end of the trail and catch a ride back to the trailhead, having that problem solved before starting out.) While it is not always practical, it is best to have transportation lined up before starting out because it may be very difficult to get a ride back to the trailhead on some occasions.

Elevation extremes: The lowest point along the Cracker Lake hike is at an elevation of 1475 meters; the highest point is 1853 meters. Keep in mind that these figures represent the elevation extremes and don't necessarily coincide with the elevations at the trailhead or destination, although there are some hikes where that is the case. While we have given all elevations in meters, elevations on the topo maps are still given in feet.

Topographic maps: If you were to purchase topographic maps covering the Cracker Lake hike, you would need three--Many Glacier, Lake Sherburne and Logan Pass. We have incorporated the relevant sections of all three maps in our book.

PRECAUTIONS

We have never had any serious problems in Glacier National Park. The worst that befell us was sometimes getting more mosquito bites than we had skin to accommodate, getting soaked several times during rain storms, and trying to look presentable enough to get a ride back to the trailhead after hiking all day. While there is always the possibility of unforseen trouble to which no one is immune, most problems can simply be avoided by planning, preparation and caution. The following list is intended to get you thinking and is by no means complete. We do not have room here to go into every conceivable problem, medical or otherwise, that you might encounter in the park. We're just anxious to make you aware of some of the most common hazards to be prepared for or--better yet--avoided. Study each item carefully, and apply it to your own situation.

1. Trails: As we have mentioned previously, trail changes do occur. While seldom a problem in Glacier, it is something to keep in mind.

Stay on established trails. Walking across fragile meadows injures delicate plant life. Leaving the trail to climb a cliff or to cross a scree slope can be asking for trouble. Glacier's rocks are mostly sedimentary, and the rock in many places is referred to by climbers as "rotten." (It has been said that mountain climbers in Glacier must often hold the mountain together as they climb.) Streambeds may be slippery, especially where there is a growth of algae. The banks along many creeks are unstable, and a fall into the swirling water below could be fatal. This is not a climbing guide. If you want to travel crosscountry, we strongly recommend that you discuss your plans with an experienced ranger first.

Limit your hiking to those trails that have been worked for the season by Park Service trail crews. Check at any ranger station for a list of trails that are free of snow and have been cleared of winter debris and damage.

2. Swimming and water hazards: The waters in the park are usually too cold for enjoyable swimming. Over the years, a number of people have drowned in the park. In fact, more people have died from drowning than from any other single cause in the park. The force of the water in many streams is much greater than it appears to be, and even a strong swimmer can be caught by the current and pulled under or swept away. The cold water greatly reduces one's normal swimming ability, even in calm water.

3. Lightning: Lightning storms may arise rather quickly in the park. Many of the trails traverse high, barren ridges where no hiker in his right mind would want to be caught, especially with the added liability of a metal pack frame and other metallic gear. Check weather reports, and plan shorter hikes if there is any likelihood of a storm. If you see a storm or lightning in the distance, pull back to a lower elevation and a place where you will be least prominent. Remember that a direct hit is not necessary for a strike to be fatal; the charge tends to spread out from wherever it strikes. Avoid sheltering under prominent objects such as high trees. Lightning can and does strike in the same place more than once. Some of the lookouts take several direct hits during a single storm. While there is no foolproof way to avoid lightning if you're caught out, you can certainly reduce the risks.

You may wish to study a mountaineering text for further details.

4. **Storms:** Electrical storms have been mentioned above. These may or may not be accompanied by heavy rain, hail, sleet or snow. Be prepared by carrying suitable raingear and warm clothing. Always have matches for starting a fire in an emergency. Also, get a waterproof cover for your pack so that the contents don't get soaked. Once we started out on the Scenic Point hike on a nice, sunny day on the 24th of June. Wildflowers were blooming, and the meadows were green. Clouds gradually moved in as we gained the top, and visibility began to diminish. Snow started to fall, but we really didn't pay much attention to it in view of the time of year. The trail was soon obliterated, and we had failed to prepare for the cold weather and chilling snow. Fortunately, we were familiar with the route back and were able to retreat without incident. About a third of a meter of snow fell during that storm, and we have since learned to expect some snow as late as July and August. We have always been better prepared since then and would not dismiss a summer storm so lightly. If you do much hiking in the park, you'll eventually get caught in a storm, so be prepared.

5. **Hypothermia:** Hypothermia is a cooling of the body temperature which, if it progresses too far, can result in death. It is usually brought on by several factors working in combination, although sometimes a single factor such as cold can bring it on. Common contributing factors are cold temperatures (not necessarily below freezing), wet skin, wet clothing, wind, fatigue, and lack of proper nutrients. When several of these factors are present, the risk of hypothermia increases.

Victims of hypothermia may not realize that their bodies are cooling. They may actually sit down, drowse off and die. Some people who have died from hypothermia actually had sleeping bags, down jackets and tents with them, but they were not aware of what was happening. Once hypothermia progresses, the victim may not

be able to recognize it or take steps to ward it off. We strongly recommend that you take a first-aid course to be thoroughly acquainted with hypothermia and its prevention or treatment. We simply do not have room to cover all of its aspects here, nor is that the purpose of this book.

Hypothermia can usually be avoided by pacing yourself and avoiding fatigue, among other things. Eat well while on the trail, and nibble on high-energy foods now and then. Frequent rest stops will also help to prevent hypothermia. Keep dry. A rain poncho should be a standard item carried on every hike. Should you get wet, dry off **fast**. Build a small warming fire if needed, and change into dry clothes. Try to limit exposure to wind because it can greatly increase the rate of heat loss from your body. Rather than carry a single jacket, try to carry clothing that can be layered (e.g., T-shirt, shirt, sweater, sweatshirt, down jacket), and have at least one layer of wool. Unlike other fabrics, wool will provide some insulation, even when wet. Once you get dry, drink a cup of hot tea or soup before continuing.

6. **Heat exhaustion:** Heat exhaustion is normally associated with warmer areas; however, Glacier has its share of warm, sunny days. Many of the trails involve strenuous exercise. Many of the highcountry trails are over very open terrain where the rocks hold the heat and there is little shade. Combined with insufficient intake of water and salt, these factors could result in heat exhaustion. Pace yourself. Wear a wide-brimmed hat and a long-sleeved shirt to protect head, neck and arms from too much sun. Drink plenty of water at regular intervals (whether you are thirsty or not), carry salty snacks and rest at sensible intervals.

7. **Drinking water:** In general, there is plenty of water in most parts of Glacier, although there may be some dry areas in the park late in the season. Always carry at least one liter of water in a good, leak-proof canteen. Many little creeks and rivulets carry clear, ice-cold water, but there is no guarantee of purity. We recommend that you treat all water before drinking it,

although we admit to taking our chances with cold, running water if it is far removed from human habitations, campsites, etc. On the other hand, we would never drink from a lake without first treating the water.

Carry water purification tablets with you. They are available from most drugstores. Dosage required to purify water varies from one product to another, so follow directions on the label. Water can also be made safe for drinking by keeping it at a full boil for at least ten minutes (somewhat impractical).

Treated water may have a slightly unpleasant taste which can be diminished by shaking the canteen and leaving the cap off for a while.

Never drink from any water source that is suspect for any reason.

8. Physical conditioning and acclimatization: These are important prerequisites for an enjoyable hike. To come from a sedentary job and immediately tackle one of the long, strenuous hikes in the park may be asking for trouble. Before researching a hiking guide, we usually jog daily for a month or two.

9. High elevations: There is less oxygen at high altitudes. Many of the hikes described in this book attain fairly high elevations where you are likely to tire more quickly. Proper pacing is important.

10. Mosquitoes and other species of flies: The combination of an effective insect repellent, long sleeves, long pants, head protection and mobility (which includes slapping motions of the arms and hands) can do a lot to diminish the insect problem. Mosquitoes usually occur in localized areas of the park throughout the summer but can often be avoided simply by moving from one place to another.

11. Snowbanks and glaciers: Don't be tempted to slide down snowbanks. It sounds like fun, but it is easy to gain too much momentum--so much that there is nothing to slow you down except a pile of jagged rocks at the bottom. We carry an ice axe on hikes where we anticipate having to cross snow, but an ice axe won't be particularly useful to anyone unfamiliar with its use.

Never venture out onto a glacier without an experienced guide. Deep crevasses are often covered by a thin crust of innocent-looking snow which could conceal a fatal drop.

12. Darkness: If you hadn't planned to spend the night out, darkness may be a hazard. Always, **always** carry matches in a waterproof container, and carry a flashlight with spare bulb and batteries. Even when planning a dayhike, be prepared to spend the night out if you should have to. Once you realize there is no way you can make it back before dark, situate yourself as comfortably as possible while it is still light enough to see. If you can't see, don't move any more than absolutely necessary.

13. Hiking alone: Although many people do hike alone, it is not recommended. (One of the pioneer climbers in the park, Norman Clyde, made a number of first ascents solo.) The potential danger of solo hiking is that a minor injury can have serious consequences if there is no one to go for help. If you can't hike with someone, at least notify a reliable individual of your intended route and expected time of return.

14. Direct sun: Your eyes and skin should both be protected from overexposure to sun. At higher altitudes, sunburn can occur very quickly, and the glare from sun on snow can result in sunblindness. We wear sunglasses at higher altitudes if glare is likely to be a problem. Goggles with special filters are recommended for anyone who might be exposed to glare for long periods of time.

Sunburn can be prevented in the traditional manner by wearing clothing that leaves as little skin exposed as possible, a wide-brimmed hat, and lotion or cream to protect what cannot be covered.

15. Injuries and illnesses: Be familiar with first-aid treatment and diagnosis for sprains, broken bones, cuts, hypothermia, sunblindness, heat exhaustion, heat stroke and other problems that may arise in the backcountry. Rangers report that the most common first-aid problem for hikers is blisters.

Prevention is the best "treatment" for blisters. Wear comfortable, broken-in footgear; don't wear lumpy socks; do carry moleskin and know how to apply it to protect a sensitive area. Always carry a complete first-aid kit.

16. Domestic animals: Horses have the right-of-way along trails. This is for the safety of both riders and hikers because if an animal should panic, it could take not only itself but nearby hikers over the brink. Some of Glacier's trails are very narrow with sheer dropoffs. If you see horses approaching, wait quietly in a safe spot beside the trail, allowing them an opportunity to pass.

17. Wild animals: Many of Glacier's animals have become very accustomed to people, especially in the campgrounds and along the trails. But remember that they are still wild. Mountain goats are strongly attracted to sources of salt, including urine and perspiration. The craving is so strong that goats have been known to actually lick the arms of perspiring hikers. While the activity may seem harmless, a startled goat may raise its head quickly and inflict serious injury with its sharp horns.

To their regret, several people have found the "gentle" park deer not so gentle when frightened, cornered, or just plain weary of too-close admiration.

Most injuries resulting from animal encounters can be easily prevented by keeping a safe distance. It's hard to resist some of the park's more appealing panhandlers, but it's a little easier if you keep in mind that they love you for your peanut butter sandwich or chocolate chip cookies.

Everyone likes bear stores--the scarier the better, it seems, because there is an abundance of them centered around the approximately 500 black and 200 grizzly bears in Glacier. These are magnificent carnivores, and this is their home where man is privileged to visit. In view of the few sanctuaries left for bears, this is as it should be.

We have very seldom seen bears while hiking, but there is always the possibility of meeting one. Members of either species could be encountered on any of the hikes described in this book.

The National Park Service is undertaking a number of studies on bears, their lives, and human-bear interactions. Hopefully this research will help to provide information leading to a reduction in people-bear encounters. These confrontations are few (especially if you consider that as many as 29,000 backcountry permits may be issued in a single season), and the occasional bad encounter comes in for reams of publicity--all bad for the bears.

We strongly recommend that you heed any warning signs posted at trailheads and other places in the park. These suggestions are for your safety and have been made as a result of careful study. They may change from time to time as more knowledge is gained from research on bear behavior.

We do not intend to go into detail about what to do if you meet a bear along a trail. That subject is thoroughly covered by Park Service literature. The leaflet, "Backcountry Tips," includes a section on safeguards to be taken when camping in bear country.

Any bear seen along a trail should be reported so that the sighting can be included in the data of the studies.

Bears are wild animals and may attack without provocation, although it is the exceptional animal that chooses to attack rather than retreat. There have been three human fatalities as a result of bear attacks in the park. They were tragic, as were the many deaths from drowning, mountain climbing, automobile accidents and heart attacks. Those who would like to see the bears done away with would also have to consider banning automobiles and fencing off the streams, lakes and mountains.

An occasional bear will be removed from an area or a trail closed down in order to avert trouble. Most trail closures are temporary, being in effect only until a potentially troublesome animal moves on or is moved by Park Service personnel. Occasionally a trail will be closed permanently in order to allow the bears some much-needed latitude. Whatever the case, it is vitally important that you heed any closure signs.

"Bear sign" consists of a number of things--tracks, droppings, excavations, clawed bark on trees. Tracks of grizzly adults tend to be very large and distinct in sand or mud. Typically, the marks of the long claws of the grizzly are farther ahead of the footprint than the claw marks of the black bear. In some instances, the claw marks may not show at all.

Grizzlies have a large hump over their shoulders which is comprised of muscles used in digging. Their long claws are also adapted for digging, and entire meadows may be gouged up by a bear or bears in search of roots, bulbs and small mammals. The freshness of the soil is often an indication of how recently the bear was at work.

Bear droppings are found along many of the park's trails and indicate to a certain extent what they have been feeding on. For instance, when the huckleberries are ripe, the droppings are usually purplish. The freshness of droppings is relatively easy to judge and is an indication of whether the bear was in the area recently or not.

Many hikers theorize that noise will help to prevent an encounter by warning the bear and giving it an opportunity to retreat. In order to avoid surprising a bear, they talk loudly, affix "bear bells" to their packs, etc. There is no guarantee that by being noisy you can avoid bears, but many are of the opinion that this practice reduces encounters considerably. (Then there are a few people who think noises may attract bears!) The Park Service brochures will reflect the current thinking on this.

While most people think "grizzly" when it comes to bear attacks, black bears should not be taken lightly. Never tease any bear or approach it closely. Never get between a sow and her cubs. If hikers report having seen a bear in the vicinity of the trail ahead, do not continue until you are sure it has moved on.

Backcountry campers should be sure to properly hang their packs and food where bears cannot reach them. Maintain a spotless camp, and never cook or have food in a tent.

HORSEBACK RIDERS AND PACKERS

This book was written with the foot traveler in mind, but many people prefer to see the park on horseback. Stock is not permitted in some areas, and some trails are not safe for horses. If you plan a horseback trip (other than one of the dayrides operated by a horse concession), find out at a ranger station what regulations govern the use of stock in the area where you want to go.

In order to reduce the impact of domestic animals on the park's fragile environment, grazing is not permitted. Stock must be provided with grain or pellets. Horses that have a tendancy to paw up the ground should be hobbled. If no hitchrack is available, tie a rope between two trees, then hitch the stock to the rope in such a way that there is no damage to the trees. Horses and mules are not permitted in campgrounds except for loading and unloading gear.

FISHING

Many people look forward to fishing in the park. Fishing is a challenge in Glacier, as more than one person has discovered, and technique and skill do count for something here. At one time, many of the park's lakes and streams were stocked with fish, but this is no longer the case. They are now treated as natural ecosystems, and whatever fish there are will be the result of natural reproduction.

The fish most sought after include cutthroat trout, rainbow trout, Dolly Varden trout, eastern brook trout, arctic grayling and kokanee salmon. Several other species are caught on occasion. Each of the various streams and lakes contain one to a few of each species, and many of the park's higher lakes have none because they freeze solid in winter or have never been stocked. For this reason, be sure to check before you set off to fish a particular lake--it may not contain any fish at all.

It is possible to look down into the deep waters of some lakes and see fair-sized cutthroats swimming by, paying absolutely no attention to your lure. They probably feed so well on food which occurs naturally that only the very skilled fisherman can even attract their attention.

We have only mentioned the fishing possibilities for several hikes because a book on the subject would cover many pages, and there isn't room here. Obtain copies of current fishing regulations from any of the visitor centers or ranger stations. Please adhere carefully to these regulations so that everyone can continue to enjoy fishing in the park.

A word of caution: Fish odors may attract bears, so be careful that no odors cling to yourself or your gear. Check current Park Service recommendations regarding disposal of fish entrails in various areas.

BACKCOUNTRY REGULATIONS

We won't reiterate all the Park Service rules and regulations applying to backcountry use, but the following are a few things that might not occur to a novice hiker.

1. All hikers who intend to have a fire or camp out must obtain a Backcountry Use Permit. There is no charge for the permit, and they are available daily from July through the middle of September at either the Apgar or St. Mary visitor centers. They may also be obtained from the following ranger stations, but some of these are not manned on a regular basis so that it would be best to check with them in early morning or late evening.

Belly River
Bowman Lake
Cut Bank
East Glacier
Goat Haunt
Kintla Lake
Lake McDonald
Logging Creek
Many Glacier

Polebridge
Two Medicine
Walton

2. No pets (including dogs), no firearms, and no vehicles of any kind are permitted on trails.

3. Campfires are permitted only in designated areas; and in some camping areas, no fires are permitted at all. We enjoy the warmth and glow of a small campfire, but we use a lightweight compact gas stove for all our backcountry cooking. It is cleaner, quicker, and eliminates the need for wood.

4. No green vegetation of any kind may be cut.

5. Never level and trench a tent site. These destructive practices will brand you as an amateur to backcountry travel.

6. All unburnable trash (including aluminum foil and burned cans) should be packed out. If everyone were to carry out a little more trash than they brought in, there would soon be no litter in the backcountry. If you see a gum wrapper on a trail, make it a habit to slip it into your pocket to be disposed of properly.

Other regulations apply, but the above should be followed whenever and wherever you camp.

Each backcountry campsite has a limit tailored to the number of people the area can sensibly accommodate. Imposing these limits helps to insure against overcrowded, messy campsites and degradation of the environment. Depending on the fragility of the area, the campground limits vary from six to forty campers. Horses are prohibited in some camping areas, and as many as ten are allowed in the vicinity of others.

All of these regulations are designed to increase the quality of your outdoor experience in Glacier.

THE METRIC SYSTEM

The universal metric system is now in use throughout the park. Our suggestion is to forget about conversions and just "think metric." The two measurements we use in this book are the **kilometer** for distances and the **meter** for elevations and very short distances. We have marked the kilometers on our maps of the trails. If you are familiar with the reading of topo maps, it is easy to determine how far you have hiked and how far it is to your destination by studying the kilometer marks. You will soon have a good concept of how much distance a kilometer represents.

Our basic maps are reproductions of the topo maps which still give elevations of contours, peaks and other features in feet. The metric measurements, where our maps are concerned, apply only to the trails.

HOUSEKEEPING

Glacier National Park is large enough to accommodate a fair number of people in its backcountry if hikers and stockmen stay on the established trails and treat the land respectfully. The following suggestions should come naturally to experienced outdoorsmen.

1. Pack out all litter. If a campfire is permitted, burn any paper and garbage that can be totally consumed by fire.

2. If no pit toilets are available, dig a small hole in the earth, well away from any lake or stream, and be sure to cover it well.

3. Never wash in a lake or stream. If you need water for washing, carry it in a clean container from the lake or stream to your campsite.

SEASONS

For most users of this book, the season is short--generally from the middle of June through the middle of September. The length of the season varies from year to year. Spring means the days start to warm, the snow to melt, and the lowland plants to grow. Wildflowers appear here and there. Most of Glacier National Park is not accessible at this time, but road crews start the long chore of opening Sun Road.

Summer is **the** season in the park. There are some spots where the snow never melts, but most of it is gone from the lower valleys, and it gradually disappears up the slopes as summer progresses. Insects, mammals, birds and plants are all taking advantage of the short growing and reproductive season. Storms occur rather frequently, usually bringing rain but sometimes bringing snow and sleet as well. Sightseers are driving the park roads; hikers and horseback riders are on the trails. Parts of the landscape are blanketed with wildflowers.

Towards the end of August or early September, light snow may appear higher up, an indication of the gradual coming of fall. Fall means cooler nights and the changing colors of maples and aspens. Many of the mammals at the higher elevations go into hibernation, and many of the birds fly south. Other animals, such as the white-tailed ptarmigan and the snowshoe hare, gradually exchange their brown coloration for white, an adaptation for survival in the winter landscape. Some mammals may remain active until fairly late in the fall, and the grizzly is one of these. Bald eagles visit McDonald Creek to feed on spawning salmon; bighorn rams gather harems and begin their battering, head-to-head combat; the bugling of elk can be heard. Gradually the snow begins to deepen on the ground, and fall turns to winter.

Winter means shorter days and longer nights. While many animals are hibernating, others, such as the pikas, live off vegetation stored during the short winter. Predators such as the lynx feed on the snowshoe hares, and an occasional wolverine may be spotted by a ranger on patrol. The highcountry is virtually inaccessible, and Sun Road is under many meters of snow in places. Cross-country skiers appear in the lowland valleys.

EQUIPMENT

Many factors must be considered when selecting equipment. What we take with us depends on the length of the hike, the terrain, the weather and other factors. There are certain basic items which all hikers should consider, and you can add or subtract items from this list to meet your personal needs. We do suggest that you buy quality products that will last for years.

Emergency kit: We have a zippered plastic container in which we carry a wide variety of items for potential use in an emergency. This kit goes with us, not only on dayhikes and backpacks, but in the vehicle as well. Here is a list of what we include in our kits, though you will want to tailor the list to meet your own needs.

Bags (large, plastic-type)
Batteries (extra set for flashlights)
Blanket (emergency-type)
Bulbs (spares for flashlights)
Can opener (small, G.I.-type)
Candies (non-melting)
Compass (quality is important)
Cord (nylon)
Dimes (for pay phones)
Elastic bandages
Fire-starting jelly (commercial compound in tube)
First-aid kit (complete enough to meet all common emergencies)
Flashlights (two small ones per person)
Glacier cream (sun screen)
Keys (vehicle--use a safety pin to attach them to the inside of your pack!)
Knee brace
Knife (pocket-type with a variety of blades)
Insect repellent
Laces (extras for boots)
Lighter (disposable, butane-type)
Lip salve (sun screen)
Match containers (two, waterproof)
Matches (paper)
Matches (waterproof)
Moleskin (for prevention or treatment of blisters)
Money ($20 bill)
Needles and thread
Notebook
Pencil
Prescriptions (extra supply in case of delay)
Razor blade (single-edge in plastic pill bottle)
Rubber bands
Safety pins
Salt tablets
Thermometer (in a case)
Toilet paper
Whistle
Wire

Dayhikes: It is possible to take off for the day with no special equipment whatsoever, but the outing may be more enjoyable (and you will be in a better position to meet certain emergencies) if at least some items are at hand. We take the following items on all hikes, no matter how short.

1. A comfortable daypack of lightweight material and good quality. Be sure it is large enough to hold all your gear.

2. Emergency kit (see description above).

3. A leak-proof canteen. (Ours are made of polyethylene and have an attached plug which cannot be easily lost.)

4. Enough emergency food, such as non-melting candies and other items, for at least one extra day in the field.

5. Comfortable, broken-in footwear. Don't break your new boots in on the trail; have that done long before you arrive in the park, and be sure that the boots have good soles and won't slip if there is snow or water on the trail. Most hikers prefer a lug sole.

6. A windbreaker, extra shirt, down sweater, gloves and stocking cap. While these may not be needed on most summer trips, they should be carried in your pack. If it gets cold (and it can, even in summer), you will be glad you brought these extra items along.

7. A rain poncho. Some of those made of newer fabrics "breathe," keeping the rain off but allowing perspiration to evaporate.

8. Long pants. We always wear long pants (usually denim) for protection from thorns and twigs, insects, and sun.

9. A wide-brimmed hat to provide shade on hot, sunny days. Be sure it provides shade for the back of your neck.

10. Sunglasses for protection from glare off snow or water.

11. This guide, maps, plant and animal field guides, fishing regulations.

12. Camera with accessories and extra film.

13. Binoculars.

14. Toilet paper.

15. Two plastic litter bags.

16. An ice axe if there is the possibility of snow along the trail.

Backpacks: Hikers of a century ago might have headed into the wilderness with little more than a bedroll and a minimum of food. Living off the land is no longer practical and is illegal in national parks. Today's backpacker should bring with him everything he may need and leave no evidence of his visit. Here is our list for a typical backpack in Glacier.

1. Everything listed for a dayhike, including the emergency kit, with the exception of the daypack itself.

2. A comfortably fit backpack of good quality. Most have a waist band which helps to distribute the weight more evenly between the hips and shoulders. Select one large enough to hold everything you need, and consider getting a waterproof cover that will protect the pack and sleeping bag.

3. A tent will add to the enjoyment of most hikes and, if equipped with a floor and rainfly, can keep you comfortable through a storm. Don't forget the tent poles, tent stakes and whatever cord is necessary to set the tent up.

4. Your choice of a sleeping bag will depend on the weather forecast. It is suggested that a sleeping bag for summer use in the park be rated for weather somewhat below freezing. It should be stored in a water-resistant stuff bag. Down is usually considered to have the best insulative value for the weight, but it is of little use when wet. You may also wish to consider the less expensive, fiber-filled bags. Some people sleep "warm," and some sleep "cool." You will have to experiment to determine your individual needs. Be sure you are prepared for cold weather in Glacier, regardless of how benign it may seem at the time.

5. A small portable stove can eliminate the need for a campfire, and open fires are prohibited in many backcountry campgrounds. There are several excellent, light-weight gas stoves on the market, and they are safe and efficient and clean if used properly.

6. Many fuel containers have a tendency to leak. Besides making your pack highly aromatic and flammable, a leaky container can ruin your food supply, so be sure to get one that won't cause problems.

7. A ground mat is imperative for warmth in cold weather and can also add to the enjoyment of many summer hikes.

8. At least twenty meters of strong nylon cord is needed for hanging packs and food beyond the reach of bears.

9. Food should be carefully planned so that weight is conserved but at no risk of running short.

10. Always carry identification in case of emergency. It will also be required if you enter Canada.

ADDITIONAL INFORMATION

A list of ranger stations has been given under "Backcountry Regulations." Additional information may be obtained by mail from:

The Superintendent
Glacier National Park
West Glacier, Montana 59936

All emergencies should be reported to a park ranger. Be prepared to provide him with any information you may have as to the nature of incident or injury, location and other facts. For newcomers to the park, we suggest that you go on one of the half-day or all-day naturalist-led hikes as an introduction before heading out on your own. The evening and campfire programs can also be informative. The stores in the park and surrounding areas carry a variety of books on the park and related subjects.

Iceberg Lake

Forest--the McDonald Valley

Spruce grouse

Sunrift Gorge

Trail in Glacier's highcountry

LIST OF TRAILS IN THIS BOOK

Hike	General Location of Trailhead	Page

AKOKALA LAKE

Summary: Starting from Bowman Lake Campground, this trail follows part of West Lakes Trail. It climbs through a forested area before dropping down to Akokala Creek. It continues from there for a short distance to a junction, then follows Akokala Lake Trail to the lake itself

Length:
  One way - 9.1 km
  Round trip - 18.2 km
Dayhike or overnight
Season: Mid June
Vehicle shuttle: No
Elevation extremes: 1253-1448 m
Topographic maps:
  Quartz Ridge
  Kintla Peak

It is suggested that you check with the ranger before making this hike because the trail is not as heavily used as some of the park trails and may be overgrown in places. (We did find the trail to be in excellent condition on the June day when we last hiked it.)

The trailhead (A; 0.0) is located at the upper/north end of the Bowman Lake Campground loop road. The first stretch is along part of the West Lakes Trail through forestation varying from lodgepole to spruce-fir. While overall elevation extremes are not great, there is a fair amount of up and down as the trail follows the west part of Numa Ridge. Wildflowers include meadowrue, bunchberry, claspleaf twistedstalk, thimbleberry and beargrass (and wild strawberries that, some years, produce a small berry that makes the larger, domestic berry taste tame). Common shrubs include Rocky Mountain maple, thinleaf alder and red-ozier dogwood. There may also be a bloodthirsty gang of mosquitoes along this trail.

A bridge crosses Akokala Creek at point B (5.4 km). The exact location of the crossing may be subject to change from time to time, witness the older bridge located a short distance downstream. The logs and trees in the creek are a clue to the creek's temperamental behavior in the past.

From the creek crossing, the trail climbs a short distance to a junction at point C (5.6 km). West Lakes Trail continues ahead from here; the trail to Akokala Lake goes to the right and climbs along a gentle slope in an open forest--predominantly lodgepoles mingled with a few firs and larches. Grasses, beargrass and numerous low shrubs combine with open forest to create a park-like atmosphere along this part of the hike. Akokala Creek can be heard but not seen from the trail. The gradual climb continues to just beyond the 9-km point, then there is a short drop to the lakeshore and trail's end at point D (9.1 km).

Akokala Lake (elevation 1443 m) is a relatively small lake. It is shallow along the shoreline at the lower end and is closely surrounded by forest. In the past, this lake has had both cutthroat and Dolly Varden trout in it.

Among the features visible from near the foot of the lake are a part of Numa Ridge, Numa Ridge Lookout (see "Numa Ridge Lookout"), Reuter Peak and Kintla Peak.

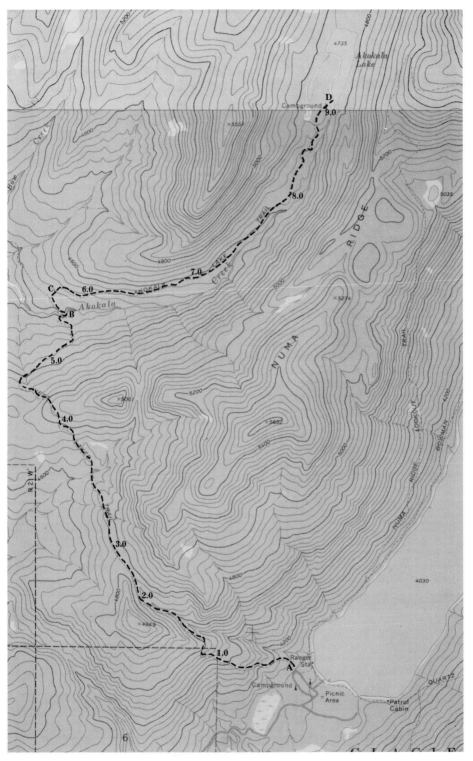

APGAR LOOKOUT

Summary: The Apgar Lookout Trail follows a closed-off road for part of the way. It starts out in a low, damp area which is gradually left behind as the trail begins to climb Apgar Mountain. At about 2.1 km, the road becomes a trail. The incentive for the long, steady climb to the top is the expansive view from the lookout.

Length:
   One way - 5.6 km
   Round trip - 11.2 km
Dayhike
Season: Mid June
Vehicle shuttle: No
Elevation extremes: 1036-1596 m
Topographic map:
   McGee Meadow

The trailhead requires a little more effort to reach than most trailheads in Glacier. Take Sun Road north from the west entrance station for 0.3 mile and turn left/west on a gravel road. Proceed a little over 0.3 mile to where the road T's, and keep to the right. Continue another 100 yards to a road fork, and keep left. In another 0.5 mile, the road crosses McDonald Creek and heads south along the Middle Fork of the Flathead River for a short distance. There is another fork 0.9 mile beyond the bridge. Keep to the right and continue 0.5 mile to a parking area in a clearing. The trail starts (A; 0.0) as a road continuing from the edge of the clearing.

There is a cable across the road near the start of the hike, and the "trail" follows the two-track road beyond the cable. Lodgepole pine, western larch and black cottonwoods thrive in the low, damp ground along the first part of the hike. (So do mosquitoes at some times of year!) Several small creeks cross the trail (road) within the first kilometer. The moisture creates a favorable habitat for both green and white bog-orchids, and Equisetum (or "horsetail") is common in the ditches beside the trail. Dense thickets of thinleaf alder occur all along here, as do thimbleberries and wild straw-berries.

The road forks several times, but the main route is quite obvious, and a few metal tags on the trees help to define it. As the road continues, it enters a dense forest of lodgepole pines. The forest floor is covered with bracken ferns early in the summer. A big fire swept through this area in 1929, and old, charred stumps can be seen in the woods. Before the fire, this area was forested by western red cedars and hemlocks. Some western larches survived the holocaust because of their thick bark, but most other species were burned out. The lodge-poles and black cottonwoods you see here now are pioneer species. If natural succession continues uninterrupted, western red cedars and hemlocks may be the dominant species of trees in some future time.

Near point B (2.1 km) the road becomes a trail as it continues uphill. Just beyond point B at 2.2 km, the trail reaches the first of three long switchbacks which climb the side of Apgar Mountain. There are some Rocky Mountain maples in the woods along here, and several open areas along the switchbacks afford nice views to the south. There is a second switchback at 3.4 km, and the third is at 4.5 km. The trail continues to climb beyond the last switchback, becoming more gradual as it nears Apgar Look-out and the radio transmitter at point C (5.6 km). A few Engelmann spruce grow along the trail near the top.

The lookout is the end of the trail, although the summit of Apgar Mountain is still a short distance away. The lookout was once manned throughout the summer seasons, but it is now occupied only during periods of high fire danger. There are some superb views of Lake McDonald from the lookout. Also included in the view are Sun Road, the Middle Fork of the Flathead and an august assembly of mountains and peaks. The scars left by a large fire can be seen to the north. These are the result of a lightning-caused fire that swept through the area surrounding Huckleberry Mountain and the Camas Creek drainage in 1967.

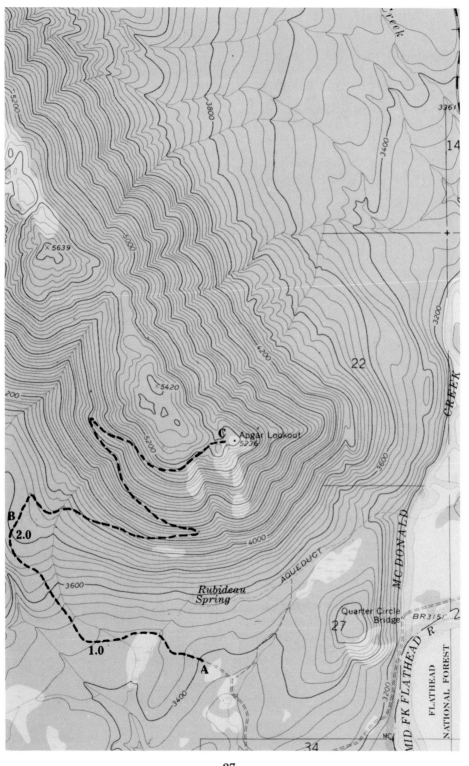

AVALANCHE LAKE

Summary: The hike to Avalanche Lake is one of the most popular in the park. An early start might insure a little more solitude, but--early or not--this is a beautiful hike. It starts at a trailhead near Avalanche Campground and climbs through a deep, quiet forest of western red cedars and western hemlocks. The ground is carpeted with moss in many places, and there are some superb views of Avalanche Creek along the first part of the hike. As the trail approaches Avalanche Lake, it drops down slightly, then parallels the lake's west shore. (This hike should not be confused with Avalanche Trail.)

Length:
   One way - 4.2 km
   Round trip - 8.4 km
Dayhike
Season: Mid June
Vehicle shuttle: No
Elevation extremes: 1048-1195 m
Topographic map:
   Mount Cannon

Parking may become congested near the ranger station at Avalanche Campground, and we suggest you park at the picnic area on the opposite side of Sun Road. To reach the trailhead, hike into the campground and, a short distance beyond the ranger station, take the first road going to the left. This was formerly the largest loop of Avalanche Campground (see map); however, it has been closed to vehicle traffic pending its conversion to a trail. Proceed for 0.3 km to the end of the old loop where a trail continues for 0.1 km to a trail fork. The trail going to the left from the fork is the Trail of the Cedars, a short but especially fine interpretive trail which heads back to Sun Road. Avalanche Lake Trail starts (A; 0.0) by taking the righthand fork.

Just 32 meters beyond point A, the trail forks again. Avalanche Trail-- not to be confused with the hike described here--goes to the right and eventually comes out near McDonald Lodge (see "Avalanche Trail"). Avalanche Lake Trail takes the left fork, climbing steeply at first, then becoming more gradual. Much of the route is through tall timber--western red cedar, western larch, western hemlock. Mosses upholster the rocks and logs and carpet the ground in many places; in others, the forest floor and the trail are deeply littered with brown needles. The trail is quite close to Avalanche Creek in several places. Rocks in the streambed have been worn into interesting shapes by the abrasive materials carried in the turbulent water. (Do not approach the sheer cliffs too closely; they may be undercut and dangerous.) Dead trees and logs have been wedged into the rocks by flood waters which occasionally tear through here.

Bracken ferns, queencup bead-lilies and foamflowers grow along the trail. Many plant species exhibit a preference for the more open areas where sunlight is more generous and they do not have to compete with the more shade-tolerant plants such as mosses. Wildflowers are scarce in the dark corners of the forest, and this is especially evident in red cedar forests where the very high canopy blocks out much of the light. Pacific yew is a common shrub along parts of this trail. It is usually one to two meters high and grows in large clumps. Its needles have small points and tend to grow out in a relatively flat plane. The new growth at the tips of the branches can usually be distinguished by its lighter color. Western paper birch--a tree with thin, light bark--grows in a couple of locations along the trail. Also look for devil's club, a shrub with large leaves and numerous spines on the stems. Among the occasional orchids to be seen is the spotted coral-root. Pathfinder is common along many of Glacier's trails. It is a composite, and the undersides of the leaves are a light green or silverish color. The tops of the leaves are a contrasting, darker green. If stepped on, they often lie with the undersides exposed. Not only do these stand out among the darker leaves, but the tips of the arrowhead-shaped leaves usually point in the direction the hiker is headed--hence the name "pathfinder." The long, distinctive cones which you may see along this trail are those of the western white pine which also occurs in this forest.

At point **B (2.0 km)** the trail is opposite Hidden Creek drainage. This deep gorge lies between Mount Cannon to its left and Bearhat Mountain to its right.

The trail leaves the dense forest at 2.8 km and heads downhill. Shrubs growing along this stretch include Rocky Mountain maple, cow-parsnip, thimbleberry and elderberry. Giant helleborine, a member of the orchid family, also grows here. At point **C (just under 3.0 km)** the trail is just to the right of the lake. A short drop down to the lake at this point will reveal an interesting log jam at the outlet and fine views of the lake, Avalanche Basin and several falls above the head of the lake, including Monument Falls. Avalanche is a fair-sized lake (elevation 1198 m). There is enough glacial flour coming into the lake from Sperry Glacier to lend an opaque quality to the water, although the color effect is not nearly so startling as it is in Grinnell or Cracker lakes. Avalanche Lake is heavily fished, with small cutthroat trout making up most of the catches.

From point C, the trail is situated a short distance above the west shore of the lake and heads toward the far end. Spruce, fir and various shrubs grow along these slopes. The calls of varied thrushes can often be heard, and a red-tailed chipmunk may whisk across the trail. (Its tail is rufous-colored underneath.) The trail ends near the upper end of the lake at point **D (4.2 km)**.

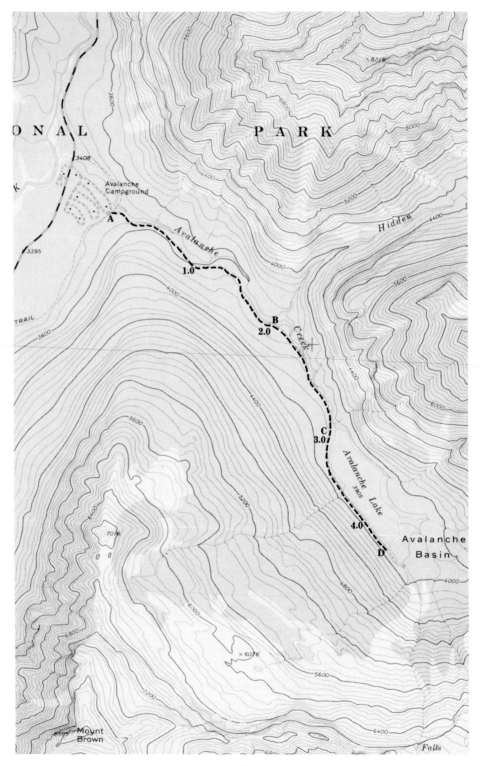

AVALANCHE TRAIL

Summary: This hike involves very little elevation change. From the trailhead near Lake McDonald Lodge, it soon heads in a northeasterly direction, skirting the lower slopes of Mount Brown. Most of the route is through a rich forest of red cedar, hemlock and larch. The trail passes near John's Lake and Moose Country Pond and ends at a junction with Avalanche Lake Trail. From there it is a short hike to Avalanche Campground. (This hike should not be confused with the "Avalanche Lake" hike.)

Length:
   One way - 9.5 km
   Round trip - 19.0 km
Dayhike
Season: Mid June
Vehicle shuttle: Yes
Elevation extremes: 988-1048 m
Topographic maps:
   Lake McDonald East
   Mount Cannon

The trailhead is reached by taking Gunsight Pass Trail which is on the east side of Sun Road. It is directly across from a road exiting the parking area at Lake McDonald Lodge. (This is also the trailhead for hikes to Snyder Lake, Mount Brown Lookout and Fish Lake.) Eighty-six meters from Sun Road there is a fork where Gunsight Pass Trail goes to the right of a fenced treatment plant. Proceed on the left fork for 63 meters to a trail junction (A; 0.0) just above the horse stable building. Avalanche Trail is the left-hand trail at this fork, and all distances are measured from here. (The right-hand trail is a branch of the Gunsight Pass Trail and soon joins the trail that continued past the fenced area.)

The trail proceeds in a northeasterly direction through a forest of elegant red cedars and hemlocks. The sunlight falls in long shafts to the forest floor, and footsteps are muffled by the deep humus. Contours of rocks and logs are softened by a wash of green moss. Devil's club, bracken fern, queencup beadlily, foamflower, bedstraw, self-heal, pink pyrola and at least one of the species of twayblade orchid grow along the trail. Light green lichens are common on the sides of many trees, and the calls of both Swainson's thrush and the varied thrush float down from the canopy. Despite its close proximity to the busy lake and Sun Road, the forest is pervaded by a solemn, quiet atmosphere.

At point B (2.3 km) a side trail goes left/west for a short distance to Sun Road; Avalanche Trail continues ahead. At point C (2.5 km) there is another junction where McDonald Creek Cutoff Trail heads left/northwest to Sun Road and McDonald Creek. Avalanche Trail continues along the right fork. Note the markers on some of the trees along the trail; these define the route for cross-country skiers.

In the vicinity of point C, conditions are drier and more open. Lodgepoles and some Douglas firs grow here, as do beargrass, ocean-spray, serviceberry, snowberry, Oregon grape, nodding onion and wild strawberry.

The trail soon re-enters the cedar-hemlock forest. There is a view of John's Lake from the 3-km point. This small lake is rather shallow, and the water becomes warm as the season progresses. It is becoming increasingly shallow as silt is washed in and the decaying vegetation from sphagnum mats settles to the bottom. Rocky Mountain pondlilies grow on the surface, and dragonflies dart back and forth, defending their territories and feeding on the wing. Sundews grow near the shore. These interesting little plants are carnivorous. Small insects which alight on the plant are trapped in a sticky secretion until they can be absorbed by the plant.

The trail continues past John's Lake to yet another trail junction at point D (a little over 3 km) where John's Lake Trail goes left/northwest for a short distance to Sun Road. Avalanche Trail continues ahead and passes by Moose Country Pond at 4.5 km. Moose do frequent this area, so be watchful.

The trail swings to the right above a gravel pit at 4.7 km and may be somewhat obscure until it re-enters the forest on the other side. The last time we made this hike, bear droppings were common along the trail between John's Lake and Avalanche Campground. Based on the size, they were probably those of black bear, although grizzlies can be expected in this area from time to time. Several of the older scats contained mountain goat hair, perhaps a winter-killed animal that the bear found at the base of a cliff or an avalanche.

Avalanche Trail continues through deep, mature forest to point **E (9.5 km)** where it ends at a junction with Avalanche Lake Trail (see "Avalanche Lake"). The righthand trail goes to the lake. To reach Avalanche Campground and Sun Road from here, proceed left for 32 meters to another fork. The trail going to the right is an interpretive trail, "Trail of the Cedars." The campground is reached by taking the left fork for 0.1 km to the campground loop. By following the road to the right for 0.3 km (see map), you come to another road which goes to the right for a short distance to the ranger station and, just beyond, Sun Road.

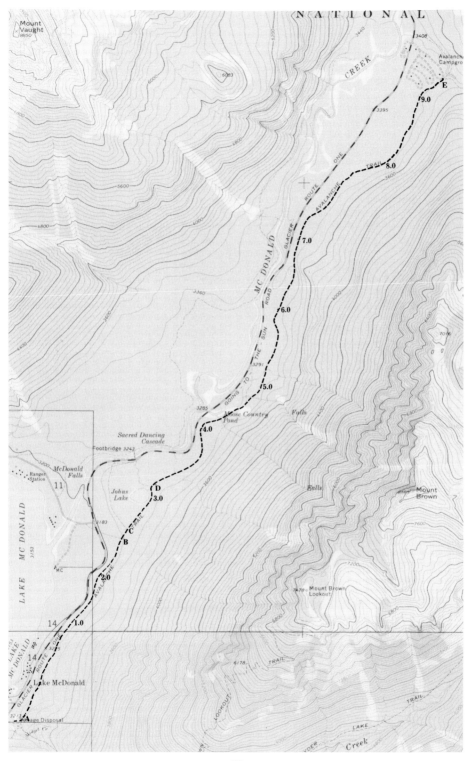

CRACKER LAKE

Summary: On a clear, sunny day, Cracker Lake is one of the most startling scenes in the park--a chalky, turquoise-blue lake in a high basin surrounded by cliffs. The trail starts near Many Glacier Hotel, swings past Governor Pond and above Lake Sherburne for a short distance, then climbs Canyon Creek drainage to Cracker Lake. The trail continues to the head of the lake where it ends among the remains of old mining equipment, including a huge ore concentrator that was never used.

Length:
    One way - 10.4 km
    Round trip - 20.8 km
Dayhike or overnight
Season: Early July
Vehicle shuttle: No
Elevation extremes: 1475-1853 m
Topographic maps:
    Many Glacier
    Lake Sherburne
    Logan Pass

The trailhead for the Cracker Lake hike is located at the south end of the parking lot above Many Glacier Hotel. The trail heads south for 75 meters to a trail fork (A; 0.0). The righthand fork goes to Piegan Pass; the lefthand fork goes to Cracker Lake.

Small subalpine firs and lodgepoles grow randomly in the vicinity of the trailhead. The route heads gradually downhill, passing to the right of Governor Pond at 0.3 km. Many shrubs border this stretch of trail--snowberry, russett buffaloberry, thinleaf alder, thimbleberry and cow-parsnip.

The trail continues downhill past Governor Pond and swings around the head of Lake Sherburne at 0.9 km. During dry years, the upper part of this reservoir may be very low or even dry. In the early 1900s the Swiftcurrent Valley area was the object of intense speculation. Some tiny seeps of oil were discovered here, and the big "oil boom" was on. Nothing of commercial quantity was found, and the boom fizzled. There was also a mining venture at Cracker Lake. A small town, complete with some buildings and a saloon, sprang up in the general area of what is now called Cracker Flats. Its heyday was behind by about 1900, and the settlement vanished.

As the trail continues around the end of Lake Sherburne, it tends to climb gradually. By now you will have noted that this trail gets quite a bit of horse traffic which puts a few minor obstacles in the path of the hiker. Flies and odors may be more bothersome than they are along trails not so frequently used by horses. At 2.2 and 2.3 km there are side trails which branch off to the left of the main trail. A small bridge crosses Allen Creek at point B (2.7 km). This creek drains two lakes with picturesque names--Falling Leaf Lake and Snow Moon Lake.

The trail switchbacks steeply uphill beyond point B. From these switchbacks there are some fine views of parts of the Many Glacier area, including Grinnell Point, Mount Wilbur, Ptarmigan Wall, Mount Henkel, Altyn Peak, Appikuni Mountain and the upper end of Lake Sherburne. Engelmann spruce and Douglas fir grow along the trail as it continues to climb.

By the time the trail reaches the 4-km point, the steep climb has tapered off and elevation is gained more gradually. The trail is above and parallel to Canyon Creek which drains Cracker Lake. A rocky talus slope at 5.1 km is a good place to look for pikas. Pikas are tiny, tailless members of the rabbit family. They are also called "alpine haymakers" because of their unusual behavior. They dry vegetation on rocks in the sun, then store it for the winter. They may squeek and disappear into the rock pile if alarmed.

At 5.5 km the trail drops down and follows the right side of the wide, rocky drainage of Canyon Creek. Flood waters have left a very apparent path through the landscape adjoining the creek.

A bridge spans Canyon Creek at point C (6.1 km). From here to Cracker Lake, the trail is above the east side of the creek, climbing steadily. Spruce and other trees grow along the route in some areas while shrubs are predominant in others. Subalpine firs and grassy slopes gradually prevail as the trail reaches higher elevations. Wildflowers are abundant. There may be a brilliant display of alpine fireweed, a low-growing species unlike the form found at lower elevations. Other flowers that are common along the trail are beardtongue, St. John's-wort, giant helleborine and Siberian chives.

The trail continues to climb to about the 9-km point. It then drops down somewhat as it passes above Cracker Lake (elevation 1801 m). The lake was named during the mining days when some prospectors left part of a lunch, including crackers, with the idea of returning later. Prior to this time, the lake was known as "Blue Lake." The water is an opaque turquoise blue. Hikers not familiar with the effects of glacial flour are often stopped in their tracks as the strange-colored lake comes into view. Glacial flour is the term used to describe rock which has been ground to a fine powder by glacial action. The material is so fine that when water from the melting glacier carries it into the lakes, it is actually suspended in the water. In large enough quantities, it can alter the natural colors of the lakes. Large amounts of glacial flour enter Cracker Lake from Siyeh Glacier which is above the upper end of the lake.

From the foot of the lake, the trail continues above the left/southeast shore. It climbs a fair distance above the water, providing vantage points for good overall views. There are a few copses of subalpine firs and willows scattered over the open, grassy meadows; and white-crowned sparrows often sing from the tops of the firs. Mount Siyeh, distinguished by a dark diorite band sandwiched between layers of low-grade marble, is above the lake to the south. Cracker Mountain is somewhat to the southeast, and Cataract Mountain can be seen somewhat to the right of the lake. Note the large terminal moraine (a pile of rocks and gravel) deposited by Siyeh Glacier.

At 9.9 km the trail climbs a short distance, going around a rocky outcropping. At 10.2 km it passes some mine tailings where there is a small rock wall and some pieces of ore-car track. The trail reaches the end of the lake at 10.3 km and drops down to end near some derelict mining equipment at point **D (10.4 km)**.

The old Cracker Mine has an interesting history. In the late 1890s, during the short-lived interest in minerals in the Swiftcurrent area, the Cracker Lead went back over a thousand feet here. But operations never went beyond the development stage, and no minerals of commercial value were taken out. The remains of a hundred-ton concentrator are rusting quietly away among the collapsed beams. Among other things were a boiler, piston and cylinder, flywheels, separator, pipes and nails.

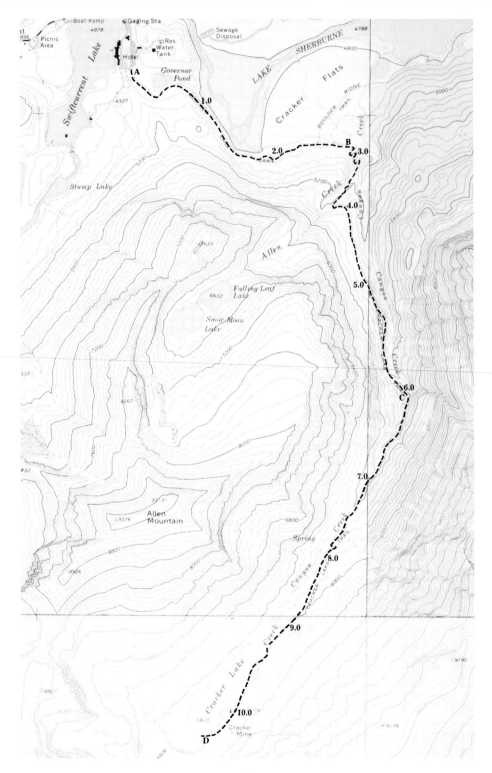

FISH LAKE

Summary: The first part of the hike to Fish Lake follows Gunsight Pass Trail, the same route covered by the first parts of the Mount Brown Lookout and Snyder Lake hikes. Each destination is different, and each makes a nice one-day hike. For that reason, we describe them as three separate hikes. The trail leaves Sun Road near Lake McDonald Lodge and climbs past the trail forks to Mount Brown Lookout and Snyder Lake. It then crosses Snyder Creek and turns from the Gunsight Trail onto Snyder Ridge Trail. Between here and the lake is one of the most beautiful woodlands in the park. And Fish Lake has a charm that the name fails to imply.

Length:
  One way - 4.7 km
  Round trip - 9.4 km
Dayhike
Season: Mid June
Vehicle shuttle: No
Elevation extremes: 975-1264 m
Topographic map:
  Lake McDonald East

The trailhead is on the east side of Sun Road across from the road exiting the parking area at Lake McDonald Lodge. (The exit road and the trailhead are 65 meters north of where Snyder Creek goes under Sun Road.)

The trail starts (A; 0.0) by following the Gunsight Pass Trail which goes to Sperry Chalets. Within 80 meters of Sun Road, the trail passes the horse stables which are to the left of the trail. At 130 meters it passes to the right of a fenced treatment plant, and Snyder Creek is close to the trail on the right. The trail climbs through a forest of tall cedars, and the roar of Snyder Creek can be heard from many points along this first stretch of the hike.

At point B (2.8 km) the Mount Brown Lookout Trail goes left (see "Mount Brown Lookout") while the trail to Fish Lake continues ahead. At point C (2.9 km) the Snyder Lake Trail goes to the left (see "Snyder Lake").

The trail to Fish Lake continues ahead here and drops down to where a wooden bridge crosses Snyder Creek at point D (3.1 km) via Crystal Ford.

Just after crossing Snyder Creek, there is one last trail junction at point E (a little over 3.1 km). Gunsight Pass Trail continues on the left, eventually reaching Sperry Chalets and Gunsight Pass (see "Gunsight Pass"). The route to Fish Lake now follows Snyder Ridge Trail which goes to the right from the junction. A short distance up the trail from point E is an old hemlock with a series of vertical, oblong holes--the work of the pileated woodpecker. This large bird is very distinctive. It has a sizeable red crest and exhibits large white areas under the wings when it flies. It is most often seen in the lower forests of the park when it flies across the road.

The trail switchbacks uphill from the junction to the 3.3-km point, then becomes more gradual. It wanders through a hemlock forest that has all the fine, intricate details of a Walt Disney production or one of Grimms' fairytales. The forest floor is strewn with the small, delicate cones of the hemlock and the giant cones of the western white pine. (Please don't collect them; they've taken years to accumulate.) There is a green glow of moss where the sunlight filters down to the forest floor, and footsteps are cushioned by hemlock needles and humus. Beargrass, huckleberries, snowberries, serviceberries and many other plants grow along the trail.

The trail crosses Jackson Creek via a wooden foot bridge at point F (4.2 km). This is a fair-sized creek early in the season, running darkly beneath logs that have fallen across it. The trail remains fairly level as it continues to Sprague Creek at point G (4.5 km). A single, wide log crossed this smaller creek the last time we were here.

Fish Lake is a short distance beyond Sprague Creek at point H (4.7 km). It is small and shallow, surrounded by forest, and Rocky Mountain pond-lilies float on its surface. (They grow in shallow lakes such as this where their roots can reach down to the muddy bottom.) When they are in bloom, large yellow flowers float among the lily pads. An occasional frog basks along the grassy shoreline, and sunken logs can be seen beneath the surface on clear days. The lake is gradually filling in. If natural succession continues, it will undoubtedly become a marsh, then a bog, then a meadow which will gradually be absorbed by the forest. There are some fish here, but they are not very tasty after the season progresses and the water warms up.

Snyder Ridge Trail (also known as Snyder Ridge Fire Trail) continues south past Fish Lake and follows Snyder Ridge. For most dayhikers, however, Fish Lake makes a good place to turn around.

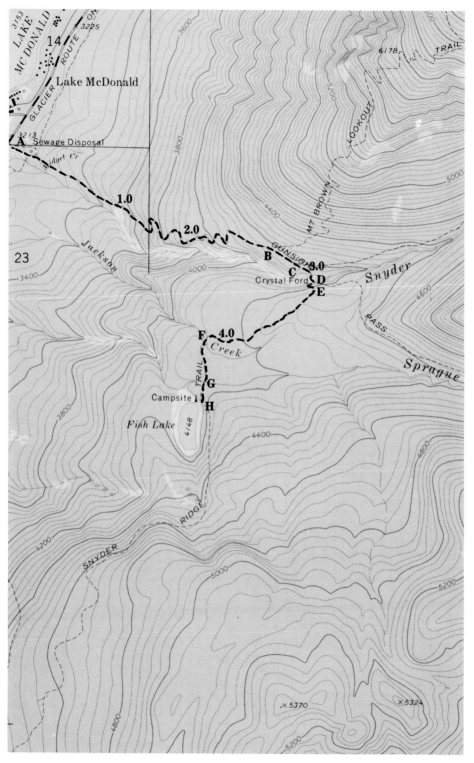

GRINNELL GLACIER

Summary: The largest glacier in the park is an exciting destination that makes this one of the most popular dayhikes in Glacier. The trail starts at a picnic area east of the Many Glacier Campground. After swinging around one side of Swiftcurrent Lake, it climbs above Lake Josephine and then far above Grinnell Lake. It then continues to climb to a picnic area near a glacial moraine. After a final steep climb up the moraine, it comes to an overlook where there are fine views of both Grinnell Glacier and The Salamander glacier. Hikers should NOT go onto the surface of the glacier unless accompanied by a park naturalist.

Length:
   One way - 8.4 km
   Round trip - 16.8 km
Dayhike
Season: Late July
Vehicle shuttle: No
Elevation extremes: 1487-1975 m
Topographic map:
   Many Glacier

The trailhead (A; 0.0) is located at the picnic area parking lot, just off Many Glacier Road between Many Glacier Hotel on the east and Many Glacier Campground on the west. This is a popular hike, and heavy foot traffic can be expected on nice days.

The trail soon enters a lodgepole forest which has come in since the 1936 crown fire which swept from the vicinity of Swiftcurrent Pass to this location in only 45 minutes. Lodgepole pine is a species which tends to come into burned-over areas. There is a spruce-fir forest across the lake which was not involved in the fire.

A bridge spans Swiftcurrent Creek, and the route soon follows the shore of Swiftcurrent Lake. Some of the trees along this first stretch have been gnawed by beavers. The higher marks were made when there was snow on the ground.

At the south end of Swiftcurrent Lake there is a trail junction at point B (a little over 1.0 km). The lefthand trail continues around the lake to the Many Glacier Hotel. The route to Grinnell Glacier heads uphill via the righthand fork. It climbs over a glacial moraine consisting of rocks and gravel camouflaged by a forest of spruce and fir. This moraine--a result of glacial activity--creates a natural dam, and Lake Josephine is backed up behind it.

After climbing the moraine, the trail drops down toward Lake Josephine at point C (1.3 km) where a short side trail goes left to a boat dock. The main trail continues above the northwest shore of the lake, passing through many semi-open areas where twinflower, cow-parsnip, mountain ash, fireweed and Rocky Mountain maple grow. The flowers in bloom vary with the seasons and the years. Even in "poor" years, the park is richly endowed with wildflowers.

As the trail proceeds above the lake, there are some ups and downs but no major elevation changes. Our progress along this part of the trail was particularly slow on one occasion when we yielded the right of way to two bighorn rams that ambled down the trail in front of us for quite some distance. There are nice views of Lake Josephine along this stretch.

There is a trail junction at point D (2.6 km). The trail to Grinnell Glacier follows the righthand fork here and keeps to the right again at point E (3.1 km) where there is another junction. The left fork drops down to a boat dock near the end of Lake Josephine, with a branch going by Grinnell Lake and on to Piegan Pass.

From the junction at point E, the trail climbs more steadily. There are a number of chartreuse-colored lichens on the rocks in the vicinity of the junction. Looking back at Lake Josephine, it is easy to distinguish the light-colored shallow water from the darker deep water. The forest in the valley to the left/south is a mature spruce-fir forest. Avalanche chutes can be seen on some of the far slopes. These are characterized by open, shrubby areas between forested slopes. The paths left by avalanches create a greater variety of habitats which account for a greater diversity of animals and plants than would be found in an area of pure forest. Moose occur in many of Glacier's valleys but are absent from the valley below due to the severe winters which occur in this area of the park.

The trail continues to climb steadily. There is a view of a hanging valley--typical of post-glacial terrain--off to the left, situated higher up than the closer valley below. Morning Eagle Falls can be seen from the trail. The sedimentary rocks along here are folded and warped in places, graphic evidence of the tremendous forces involved in mountain building. The greenish-colored rock is Appikuni mudstone; the reddish-colored rock situated higher up is Grinnell mudstone.

Farther along, the trail passes to the north of Grinnell Lake. The unusual turquoise color is caused by fine particles of glacial flour suspended in the water. This "flour" is actually rock which has been pulverized to a fine powder by the action of Grinnell Glacier. Some of the other features visible as the trail climbs toward the glacier include Grinnell Falls, Allen Mountain, Pyramid Peak, Piegan Mountain, Angel Wing and Mount Gould.

At 4.8 km are the first of several switchbacks. Three glaciers--Gem, Grinnell and The Salamander--all come into view as the trail continues. There is a lateral moraine visible to the right of Grinnell Glacier. The terrain becomes more open. It is often easy, with the help of binoculars, to pick out bighorn sheep and mountain goats on the surrounding cliffs. Rivulets of icy water trickle across the trail, and snowbanks may exist well into summer. Lake Sherburne is visible down the valley below Lake Josephine. In the distance beyond Sherburne is the Blackfeet Reservation and Duck Lake.

The trail stops its steady climb just before the 7-km point and is a little more gradual from here to the picnic area at point F (7.4 km). Subalpine firs, limber pines and arctic willows grow in the vicinity of the picnic area. It sits at the base of a lateral moraine inhabited by a clan of lunch-stealing marmots and Columbian ground squirrels. Some are aggressive and downright demanding, but--for their well being ·and yours--do not feed them.

From the picnic area, the trail goes left for a short distance and climbs steeply up the moraine. Note the rocks of various sizes which are typical of moraines. This pile of rocks was pushed to the side of the glacier, hence the name "lateral" moraine. Glaciers often build piles of rocks along their leading edges which are known as "terminal" moraines. Even after a glacier has receded or completely disappeared, geologists can often determine the extent of its forward movement by studying the moraines.

The trail reaches the glacier overlook at point G (7.8 km). This is the end of the hike as we describe it. The trail continues another 0.6 km from the overlook to the glacier, but do not go onto the surface unless accompanied by a park naturalist. A fall into a hidden crevasse could be fatal.

Grinnell Glacier covers 121 hectacres (about 300 acres), which makes it somewhat larger than Sperry Glacier and the largest in the park. Above and to the right of Grinnell is The Salamander. These were once a single glacier, but--due to warming trends--they became smaller and eventually separated.

Grinnell Glacier is named after its discoverer, George Bird Grinnell. Glacier National Park is so named because glaciers helped to form most of its features, including the characteristic U-shaped valleys. There are some fifty glaciers still in the park. Numerous glacial features can be seen out on the glacier itself, including crevasses, glacial wells and glacial tables. But again, do not be tempted to explore the surface unless you are with a park naturalist.

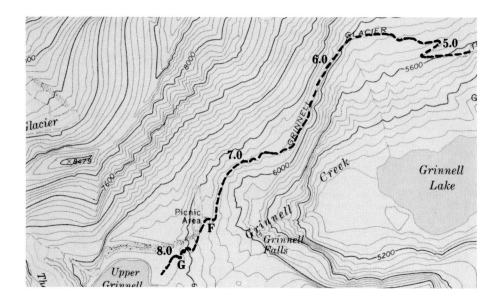

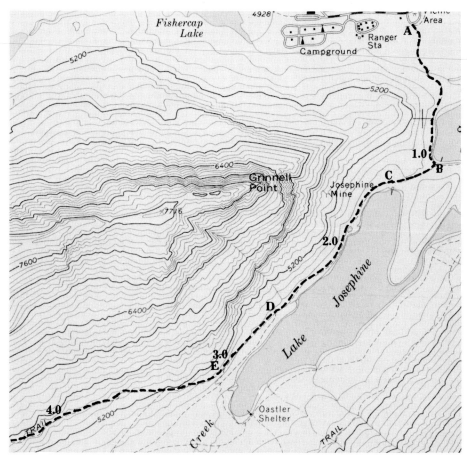

GUNSIGHT PASS

Summary: This is a long hike, and virtually everyone prefers to make it as an overnight trip. It can be done in a single day by getting an early start and maintaining a fair pace over rugged terrain. As with other hikes requiring vehicle shuttles, it is suggested that you make prior arrangements for a ride back to the trailhead. The trailhead is along Sun Road east of Siyeh Bend. The first part of the hike follows Piegan Pass Trail which drops down to Deadwood Falls; the remainder of the hike follows Gunsight Pass Trail. Enroute to Gunsight Lake there is a side trail to Florence Falls, then a long climb from Gunsight Lake to Gunsight Pass before dropping toward Lake Ellen Wilson. After swinging around the lake, the trail climbs to Lincoln Pass, then drops down to Sperry Chalets. It then continues to Sun Road where it ends opposite Lake McDonald Lodge. This trail passes through some prime mountain goat habitat.

Length:
   One way - 31.7 km
Long dayhike or overnight
Season: Mid July
Vehicle shuttle: Yes
Elevation extremes: 979-2149 m
Topographic maps:
   Logan Pass
   Mount Jackson
   Lake McDonald East

The trailhead is along Sun Road between Siyeh Bend to the west and Sunrift Gorge to the east. It is signed, and there are two parking pullouts along the south side of the road. The trailhead (A; 0.0) is near the east end of the lower pullout. The first section of this hike diagonals downhill from the trailhead (along the Piegan Pass Trail) through a mature Douglas fir-Engelmann spruce forest. After a rapid descent, the grade becomes more gradual as it continues to point B (1.8 km). Deadwood Falls is just to the right of the trail here, and Reynolds Creek has carved out the red mudstone to produce some interesting formations in the creek bed. Water cascades over several drops, and there is a nice, deep pool between the upper and lower parts of the falls. Dippers can usually be seen as they fly up and down the creek.

Piegan Pass Trail continues to a junction with Gunsight Pass Trail at point C (1.9 km). This hike follows Gunsight Pass Trail from here, heading to the right/south to a bridge across Reynolds Creek at a little over 1.9 km. The trail then passes through forest, staying north of the St. Mary River. Look for elk in the clearings among the large willow thickets along the river. Early morning and late afternoon are good times to watch for them. The trail passes to the right/north of Mirror Lake at 4.5 km.

There is a trail junction at point D (6.3 km) where Florence Falls Trail goes to the right/northwest for 1.3 km to a high falls that comes down over a series of small ledges. This is worth the side trip if you have time. Sometimes this trail may be overgrown in places. It climbs gradually at first, then steeply as it nears the falls. (The distances given for Gunsight Pass Trail do not include the 2.6-km round trip to Florence Falls.)

From point D, the Gunsight Pass Trail continues through forest. At about 7.3 km, the trail climbs steadily along the lower slopes of Fusillade Mountain. There are many open areas along here with views of Jackson Glacier, Citadel Mountain, Mount Logan, Blackfoot Glacier and Mount Jackson. Purple monkey-flowers and wood forget-me-nots grow along the trail. The grade lessens at about 9.3 km. There are some large willow thickets to the right of the trail and a fine view of Gunsight Pass ahead. At point E (9.6 km) a short side trail goes left to a patrol cabin. There are some nice open meadows at the foot of the lake. A bridge crosses the St. Mary River at the outlet of the lake at point F (9.9 km). Gunsight is a beautiful, fair-sized lake known to fishermen for its elusive rainbow trout.

There is a trail fork a short distance

south of the outlet at point **G (10.0 km)**. The left fork goes about 20 meters to another junction where a trail goes left to the site of the now-razed shelter cabin indicated on the topo. Gunsight Pass Trail follows the right fork from the junction at point **G** and climbs steadily above Gunsight Lake. Shrubs are common along the lower reaches of the climb, but the terrain becomes more barren as elevation is gained. The trail has been blasted out of rocky cliffs in places, and some of the perennial snowbanks along the trail may persist well into the season. Many rivulets of icy water flow across the trail.

Gunsight Pass (elevation 2117 m) is at point **H (14.4 km)**. There is a rock shelter cabin here, in an area frequented by Columbian ground squirrels, golden-mantled ground squirrels and mountain goats. The goats are often rather seedy looking during the summer when they shed their winter coats. Tufts of white goat hair cling to shrubs and rocks along the trail. Mountain goats are attracted to sources of salt, and a number of them can usually be seen at a natural salt lick just south of U.S. 2 along the park's southern boundary. Here at the pass, they are attracted to the salt in human urine and perspiration. They have been known to lick the perspiration off hikers' arms, but these are still wild animals, and--if startled--may lift their heads suddenly. The sharp horns can easily penetrate human flesh, so admire them from a distance and don't encourage them.

The trail drops down from the pass, and there are fine views of Lake Ellen Wilson below--a large, dark lake which occasionally yields some eastern brook trout. There are a number of switchbacks along this section of the hike (more than the topo map indicates), and the steep slope is sparsely vegetated. The trail doesn't drop down to the shoreline of the lake but proceeds above the lake and around its head before swinging above its northwest shore. Mountain goats can often be spotted along the slopes above the trail. At point **I (17.2 km)** a side trail drops to the left, down toward the lake.

The trail climbs diagonally along the slopes. At 18.5 km it is directly above the foot of the lake. At about 19 km it levels out in an interesting landscape of rocks, subalpine firs and grass. Both mountain goats and pikas are common in the area. The trail, after following a gradual grade, climbs to Lincoln Pass at point **J (20.2 km)**. Lincoln Peak is a short distance to the south of the pass, and part of Lake McDonald can be seen far below.

From Lincoln Pass the trail drops steeply via a series of switchbacks. It passes a small pond at 20.8 km and Sperry Chalets at point **K (21.3 km)**. A short distance farther, a side trail goes to a patrol cabin. At point **L (21.8 km)** the Sperry Glacier Trail goes to the right to Sperry Glacier; Gunsight Pass Trail continues left. It crosses Sprague Creek at point **M (22.1 km)**, then proceeds above the creek as it drops downhill. Along the slopes are several avalanche chutes cluttered with downed and leaning trees. Beaver Medicine Falls is off to the left at 23.7 km. The trail passes through a spruce-fir forest where an occasional Pacific yew grows in the form of a large shrub. The big pine cones along the route have fallen from western white pines. As the descent continues, western red cedar, western larch and western hemlock become common.

There is a junction at point **N (28.6 km)** where Snyder Ridge Trail--a fire trail--goes left (see "Fish Lake"). Gunsight Pass Trail keeps to the right at this junction and almost immediately crosses Snyder Creek at Crystal Ford. It then climbs to another junction at point **O (28.8 km)** where Snyder Lake Trail diagonals to the right and heads for the lake of that name (see "Snyder Lake"). Gunsight Pass Trail continues downhill from point O, proceeding above and somewhat north of Snyder Creek. At point **P (29.0 km)** Mount Brown Lookout Trail takes off on the right (see "Mount Brown Lookout"). Gunsight Pass Trail continues down to Sun Road at point **Q (31.7 km)** across from Lake McDonald Lodge.

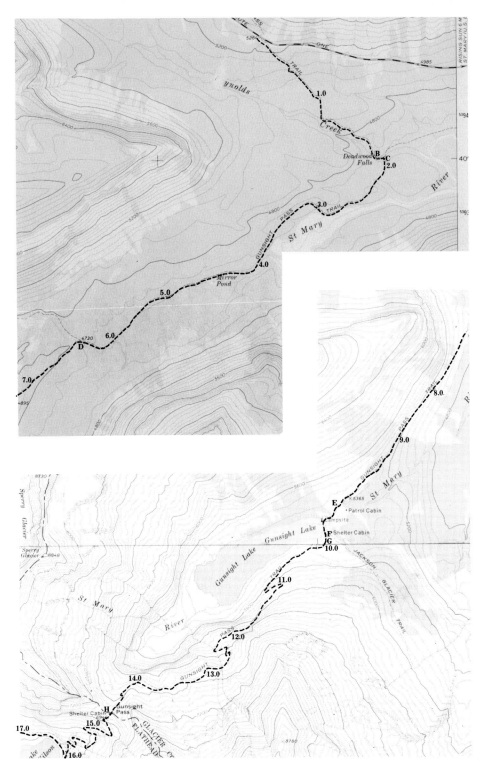

45

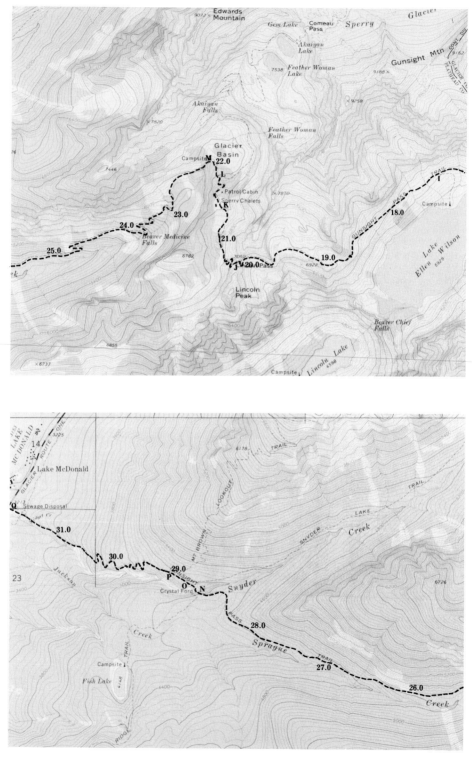

HARRISON LAKE

Summary: The trailhead is near the old Doody Homestead and can be reached by fording the Middle Fork of the Flathead River or by taking the Boundary Trail from near park headquarters to the trailhead. The route described here involves crossing the river. The trail climbs steeply at first, then more gradually to Harrison Lake. It then proceeds to the upper end of the lake. Most of the hike is through forest.

Length:
  One way - 9.1 km
  Round trip - 18.3 km
Dayhike or overnight
Season: Late July
Vehicle shuttle: No
Elevation extremes: 1005-1146 m
Topographic maps:
  Nyack
  Lake McDonald East

A fair amount of effort is required to reach the trailhead for this hike. There is often no access via the route described until late in the season--perhaps not at all. It is strongly advised that prior inquiry be made either at park headquarters or at the Walton Ranger Station to ascertain the height of the river and whether or not it is low enough to wade. (The alternative access by way of the Boundary Trail involves an 11.6-km hike from near park headquarters, which makes a very long round-trip hike!)

The river crossing is reached by taking U.S. 2 east from West Glacier for 6.4 miles to where a somewhat obscure road diagonals left. (This turnoff is 0.8 mile east of milepost 159 between mileposts 159 and 160 and can also be reached by following U.S. 2 around the south end of the park from East Glacier.)

Follow the turnoff road downhill and park in the open area. Just after the road reaches the bottom of the hill, there are railroad tracks which must be crossed on foot. Beyond the tracks, a narrow trail, which may be overgrown, heads to the river. This trail is immediately to the right of a lone black cottonwood in a thicket of trees.

Fording the river, as mentioned before, requires previous inquiry and considerable caution. The river is frequently too high to ford safely; a boat or raft might be considered. Boots or a backpack filled with water could put even an excellent swimmer at a fatal disadvantage. In addition to strong currents, the water is cold and could significantly reduce normal swimming ability if footing should be lost. The rocks on the bottom may be very slippery. In addition, the clear water is very deceptive, and what appears to be relatively shallow water may actually be rather deep. If there is any indication that the water is too fast or too deep, wait until another day before attempting the ford. Always unbuckle belts and be prepared to slip out of your pack. Many hikers carry tennis shoes and stash them on the opposite side, keeping their boots dry for the rest of the hike. Not having tennis shoes, and not wanting wet boots, we crossed barefoot.

The channel near the ford has changed since the topographic map was produced in 1964, and it will most certainly change many times again. The approximate location of the new channel is indicated by stippling; the approximate route we took to the trailhead is indicated by dots. Cross the river and bushwhack to the Boundary Trail. The Harrison Lake trailhead should be a short hike to the right on the Boundary Trail. There are several possible variations of the route to the trailhead, and willow thickets may confuse the project to some degree.

Distances in the text and on the map are measured from the trailhead (A; 0.0) which is close to the old Doody Homestead. A run-down cabin and some farm implements (plow, disc, tractor) are still around. A surprising variety of trees are found in this area, including lodgepole pine, Engelmann spruce, western white pine, western red cedar, black cottonwood and western larch. There is at least one more place along the trail to Harrison Lake where this odd assortment of trees is contained in a small area.

From near the trailhead, the trail climbs fairly steeply for about 0.4 km. It passes through a burn area where the large western larches have dark, singed bark. The thick bark of this particular species of tree usually makes it more resistant to fires than most other trees. Lodgepoles, which typically come into burned areas, are the dominant species in many places. The dense growth pattern of the lodgepoles in some places is known as "doghair." Among the plants growing on the forest floor are beargrass and Northern twinflowers.

From about the 0.4-km point, the trail becomes more gradual as it continues through the forest. Harrison Creek is off to the right/south of the trail and can often be heard in the background.

At 3.4 km there is another area where a great variety of mature trees can be found. Included are western larch, Douglas fir, black cottonwood, thinleaf alder, Rocky Mountain maple, western red cedar, western hemlock, western white pine and Engelmann spruce. (This is one of the few trails described in this book where western paper birch is found.) There may be other trees, but all of these were noted by casual observance from the trail. It would be interesting to see the results of a study to determine why so many species occur in such a limited area.

The trail reaches the foot of the lake at point **B (4.8 km)** which is opposite the outlet, then proceeds along the northwest shore of the lake. There are many fine views of the lake. By scanning the open water with binoculars, you may be able to pick out a common loon. Listen for its laughing call, especially at night.

The Harrison Lake patrol cabin (for official use only) is next to the trail at point **C (8.7 km)**. It is used by park rangers on patrol. In winter, they come here on snowshoes or-- more often--on cross-country skis. The trail continues from the cabin to the upper end of the lake at point **D (9.1 km)**. This is the end of the maintained trail, although a trail used to continue on up the Harrison Creek drainage from here. That trail is no longer maintained and is badly overgrown.

There is a picturesque gravel beach at the inlet to the lake. Fishing may be fairly good at this spot as the trout concentrate where aquatic insects and crustaceans are kept in motion by the currents. Both cutthroat trout and Dolly Varden trout are found in the lake. Eastern brook trout may still be here, although we didn't catch any. There are willow thickets here, and forest comes down to the edge along most of the shoreline except for a few places such as this upper end. Harrison Lake is a long, narrow lake, typically a dark blue-green.

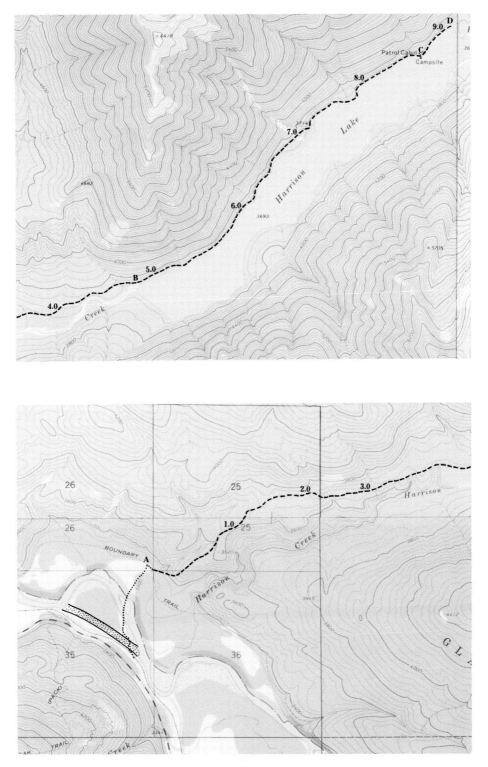

49

HIGHLINE TRAIL

Summary: This popular hike is near the Continental Divide for part of its route, and much of the first section from Logan Pass to Granite Park Chalet is above timberline. Views from the trail are impossible to do justice on paper. The hike described here follows the Highline Trail to Granite Park Chalet, then the Granite Park Trail to its end at "The Loop" along Sun Road. The wildlife and wildflowers woven into the highcountry landscape make this a choice hike. We saw mountain goats, bighorn sheep, marmots and pikas. Occasionally a grizzly may be seen; certainly the landscape calls for one whether it is there or not.

Length:
   One way - 18.6
Dayhike or overnight
Season: Early July
Vehicle shuttle: Yes
Elevation extremes: 1310-2219 m
Topographic maps:
   Logan Pass
   Many Glacier
   Ahern Pass

The trailhead (A; 0.0) is across Sun Road from the entrance to the parking lot at Logan Pass Visitor Center. (This pass is on the Continental Divide.) The trail is bordered by grassy meadows and wildflowers. Glacier-lilies may be particularly abundant, depending on the season. The nodding yellow flowers bloom in the wake of receding snowbanks, flowering higher on the hillsides as the season progresses. Look for Columbian ground squirrels and marmots in the meadows.

Several interesting features can be seen from the first part of the trail. As you stand facing north near the trailhead, Clements Mountain and Mount Oberlin are to the left/west, Pollock Mountain is ahead/north, and Reynolds Mountain is to the rear. The large snowfield on the side of Clements Mountain was once a glacier, but it has receded due to a warming trend in the climate. The jagged pro-files of peak after peak stretch along the Continental Divide to the north.

The trail drops down from the trailhead and levels out somewhat. At about 0.4 km there is a long cable anchored to the rock wall for the next 0.3 km. There are sheer cliffs here, and the cable provides a helpful handhold, especially on windy days. Going-to-the-Sun Road is below, and there are many fine views of its sinuous climb to Logan Pass. This road was opened in 1933 and was considered a major achievement of its day.

The trail ahead passes through a variety of habitats--steep, grassy slopes; a number of talus slides and rock piles; occasional patches of subalpine fir. In other places there are thickets of shrubs which include thin-leaf alder, willows, cow-parsnip, elderberry and meadowsweet. Urged on by four different field guides, we found the wildflowers easy to identify--yellow columbine, elephanthead, several species of Indian-paintbrush, St. John's-wort, nodding onion, beardtongue, pleated gentian, meadow death-camas and roundleaf alumroot. Little trickles of icy water cross the trail, and footing may be slippery in the wet places or where algae is growing.

The trail gradually climbs, passing Pollock Mountain and Bishops Cap. Mountains along the Divide form a more or less continuous ridge here that is known as "The Garden Wall"-- a very appropriate name, at least during the short growing season.

There are some excellent opportunities to see wildlife along here. Mountain goats can usually be spotted high on cliffs of The Garden Wall. (A pair of binoculars may be helpful.) There is often a small band of bighorn sheep near the trail in the vicinity of Haystack Butte. Pikas live in rockslides along this trail, especially in those where there are large, angular boulders. Listen for their distinctive squeeks, or just sit patiently near a rockslide until the pika population comes to life. The trail passes through prime grizzly country. If you are fortunate enough to see one, don't attempt anything so foolish as trying to get closer for a picture or a better view. It would be difficult to make this hike without hearing (and probably seeing) several hoary marmots. Some are relatively tame but should not be fed. Not only is the practice illegal, but it creates an artificial dependence on man. Many of those animals which accept handouts don't make it through the long winter. And there is always the danger of being bitten.

The trail crosses a big snowbank at 4.9 km. Not far beyond the bank (at the 5-km point), the trail starts to climb via a long switchback just east of Haystack Butte. We once started up this switchback in sunny weather only to find ourselves enveloped in clouds not far from the top. Visibility dropped to about ten meters, and lightning began zinging around our ears. We have an indelible memory of a ghostly-looking band of bighorn sheep, placidly chewing their cuds beside the trail as we scrambled back down. (We retreated to Logan Pass and did the hike again the next day.) The switchback ends at point B (5.6 km) at a broad, rocky saddle.

From the saddle, the trail continues to climb along the slopes of Mount Gould and The Garden Wall. There are great views of the peaks and snowfields of the Livingstone Range to the north. The trail continues its climb along steep slopes and cliffs to point C (6.6 km). This point, at about 2219 meters, is the highest elevation reached on this hike. Bird Woman Falls is across the valley.

On the right/east side of the trail at point C, there is an excellent example of fossilized algae. These colonial plants occur in a number of places in the park and once grew in a shallow inland body of water known as the Belt Sea.

From the high point, the trail drops steadily down through an area of cliffs and grassy slopes where entire hillsides may be covered with beargrass. These members of the lily family are considered to be the Park Flower. They bloom early in the season at lower elevations, such as near park headquarters, and gradually work their way up the slopes as the season progresses. At some higher elevations, they do not bloom until August. There are "good," "bad" and "so-so" years for beargrass blooms. In a "good" year, the beargrass is one of Glacier's most memorable sights.

At about the 7.7-km point, there is an area where there are a number of spire-shaped subalpine firs. Granite Park Chalet first comes into view a short distance beyond at 7.9 km. As the trail continues toward the still-distant chalet, there are many places where grizzlies have excavated the meadows in search of bulbs, roots and small mammals. At point D (10.4 km) the old Alder Trail enters from the left. This trail used to join the Highline Trail with Sun Road, but it has been abandoned to allow grizzly bears--which were often encountered along this trail--a larger area of undisturbed habitat.

At point E (10.9 km) The Garden Wall Trail diagonals uphill to the right/east to Glacier Overlook, from which there are views of Grinnell and Salamander glaciers. The Highline Trail continues ahead from point E to another junction at point F (12.0 km). There are several trails in the area which can be somewhat confusing, but Granite Park Chalet is an obvious landmark from which to get bearings. There is a short trail going from the junction up to the rock-and-log chalet which is open for only a few months out of the year. The Highline Trail continues north from the chalet area and heads toward Fifty Mountain. The hike described here leaves the Highline Trail at point F and heads downhill/southwest along the Granite Park Trail which passes below and to the left of the chalet.

In the vicinity of this last junction, there are ancient ripple marks preserved in the red mudstone. The trail passes through many small, grassy meadows dotted with thickets of subalpine fir. There are several side trails going off to the right along the trail below the chalet, but the main trail is obvious. As it continues its descent, the vegetation changes. Shrubs such as giant helleborine, cow-parsnip and thimbleberry grow in abundance. Where growth is dense, be careful not to surprise a feeding bear. The light-colored, spotted butterflies belong to the genus "Parnassius" and are related to swallow-tail butterflies.

In general, the trail descends steadily. Subalpine fir gives way to Douglas fir and Engelmann spruce. Other trees which grow here and there along the trail include western paper birch, black cottonwood and lodge-pole pine.

At point **G (17.7 km)** a trail goes to the right to Packer's Roost, a staging area for horse parties. The Granite Park Trail follows the left fork from the junction and continues (with some uphill stretches) to point **H (18.4 km)**. Here a bridge spans a pretty creek which drains the Granite Park area. The hike ends at "The Loop," a section of Sun Road, at point **I (18.6 km)**.

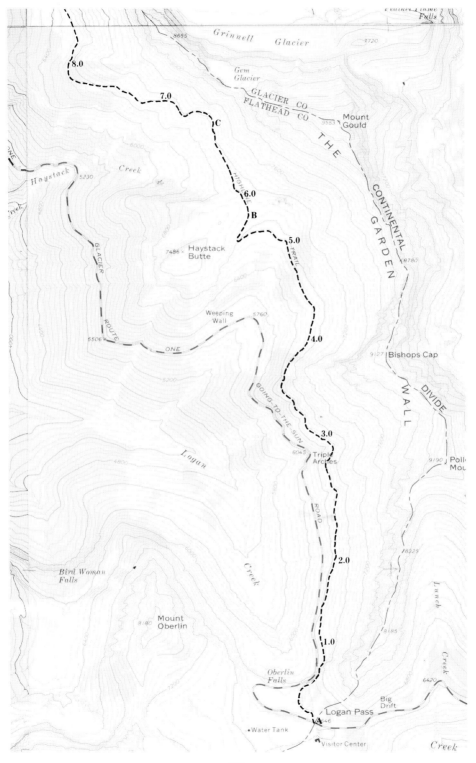

Grinnell Glacier

8.0

Gem Glacier

7.0

GLACIER CO
FLATHEAD CO

Mount Gould

C

THE

HIGHLINE

6.0

B

5.0

TRAIL

CONTINENTAL

Haystack Butte
7486

Creek

Haystack
5230

GLACIER

Weeping Wall
5760

4.0

GARDEN

Bishops Cap

ROUTE

ONE

5506

5200

GOING TO THE SUN

3.0

Triple Arches
6045

WALL

DIVIDE

Poll
Mou

Logan

4800

2.0

ROAD

18328

Bird Woman Falls

Lunch

Mount Oberlin
8180

1.0

Creek

Creek

Oberlin Falls

6420

Logan Pass
546

Big Drift

Water Tank

A

Visitor Center

Creek

53

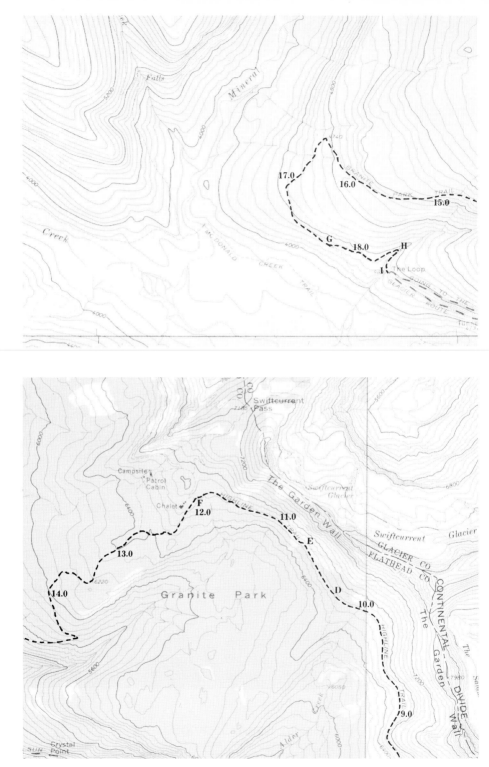

Spruce seedling

Suspension bridge--Red Eagle Creek

Along trail to Grinnell Glacier

Red Eagle Lake

Highline Trail near Continental Divide

Creek in forest near Fish Lake

Thimbleberries

Numa Ridge Lookout

Devil's Club--Quartz Lake Trail

ICEBERG LAKE

Summary: From a trailhead near the Swiftcurrent Motor Inn and cabin complex, this hike follows Ptarmigan Trail along the lower slopes of Mount Henkel. Soon after passing Ptarmigan Falls, it goes left at a trail fork and climbs along Iceberg Lake Trail, then drops down to the lake itself. Iceberg Lake is aptly named, often banked with snow and congested with floating ice until well into the season.

Length:
  One way - 7.6 km
  Round trip - 15.3 km
Dayhike
Season: Mid June
Elevation extremes: 1512-1878 m
Topographic map:
  Many Glacier

The hike to Iceberg Lake is extremely popular, and many hikers can be anticipated if the weather is good. The trailhead is somewhat obscure and most easily found by studying the topographic map. It is reached by hiking up the road which heads northwest from a point just east of the Swiftcurrent Coffee Shop and Campstore. (This building is near the end of the Many Glacier Road.) Keep to the left as the road loops through a cabin area. The trailhead (A; 0.0) is situated at the upper left/northwest part of this loop.

There are several trail forks near the start of this hike. To avoid confusion, study the map carefully. The first junction is about 20 meters beyond the trailhead. The lefthand trail goes to Swiftcurrent Pass (see "Swiftcurrent Pass"); take the righthand fork which heads uphill. A short distance farther, at a little over 50 meters, follow the lefthand fork which continues uphill (the trail to the right goes to Many Glacier Hotel).

The trail now heads steadily uphill, passing through open areas and a few patches of lodgepole pine and aspen. It crosses a two-track road at point B (a little over 0.2 km) and continues uphill. At point C (0.4 km) there is

another junction where the trail to Iceberg Lake goes left (another trail heading toward Many Glacier Hotel goes right). The steep uphill climb ends here, and the grade becomes more gradual.

The trail skirts along the lower slopes of Mount Henkel. Grinnell Point, Mount Grinnell, Pyramid Peak, Mount Wilbur, the Ptarmigan Wall and Mount Henkel can all be seen from along here. The slopes are a patchwork of grasses and shrubs such as serviceberry and pin cherry. The butterflies are as brilliant and almost as numerous as the wildflowers in Glacier. Look for the "Parnassius" (a widespread group found at higher elevations and far to the north), blues, coppers and checkerspots. While the park's insects are somewhat upstaged by mountain goats and marmots, they are another interesting facet of the environment. Many of them have become specially adapted to the harsh climate and short seasons.

As the trail continues, it leaves Swiftcurrent drainage and traverses the slopes above Wilbur Creek. At about 2.9 km the trail enters an area of small spruces, firs and lodgepoles. The Ptarmigan Wall dominates the view ahead, with Mount Wilbur rising above on the left across from Wilbur Creek. Iceberg Lake Trail can be seen ahead where it crosses an open slope.

Just beyond the 4-km point, the trail passes Ptarmigan Falls. The water drops in several increments and is very pretty when viewed from above. The trail swings around the top of the falls, and a bridge spans Ptarmigan Creek at 4.1 km. The trail is still in a spruce-fir-lodgepole forest. At point D (4.3 km) there is a trail junction. The right fork is a continuation of the Ptarmigan Trail and goes to Ptarmigan Tunnel and on to Elizabeth Lake. The left fork is the Iceberg Lake Trail.

At about 5.1 km the trail leaves the forest and proceeds along the slopes of the Ptarmigan Wall. Shrubs and small subalpine firs grow here, as do grasses and wildflowers. Beargrass is especially common. As the trail continues, note the basin ahead which is the setting for Iceberg Lake. Mountain goats can often be seen balancing nimbly on ledges of the sheer cliffs above.

The trail crosses Iceberg Creek at point **E (7.1 km)**, then continues uphill for a short distance before dropping down at 7.2 km. It passes to the left of a pale blue lake while crossing a meadow embroidered with yellow buttercups and glacier-lilies. Please keep to the trail. While these plants grow defiantly under harsh conditions, a glacier-lily crunched beneath a boot may not bloom and reproduce next year. The growing season in these high meadows is just too short for a plant to recover from crushing or bruising. Other flowers which may dot the landscape along the trail include mitrewort (a strange, intricate flower that resembles a miniature tracking station) and red mountainheath. These flowers of the high subalpine and alpine areas of the park are our favorites. They are usually small plants with tiny flowers. Surely their colors are no brighter than those of other flowers, but displayed among barren rocks or on the springy turf of a high meadow, they seem brighter by contrast.

The trail drops down through meadows and dark copses of subalpine fir to the edge of Iceberg Lake at point **F (7.6 km)**. The milky-blue lake lies in an austere basin formed by the sheer cliffs of Mount Wilbur and the Ptarmigan Wall. When we were here on the Fourth of July, there were some fair-sized patches of snow on the far side of the lake, and the water was choked with large hunks of floating ice. Glacial flour suspended in the water partially accounts for the whiteish cast to the water. The lake remains cold throughout the season, and no fish live in it--despite talk of the legendary "fur-bearing" trout. On a calm day, the snowbanks and cliffs are reflected upon the lake's surface in a way that only the hiker who has been there can appreciate.

We're harping on a theme here, but don't trample what little vegetation there is. We picked the warm side of a rock to sit and watch the ubiquitous Columbian ground squirrels and the progress of some climbers working their way up Iceberg Notch. This is a steep, narrow snow chute to the right of the lake which is often used by climbers (equipped with ropes, ice axes, crampons and considerabale experience) heading for the top of the Ptarmigan Wall. We watched the dark specks of the climbers move slowly up the white chute on the right and the white specks of mountain goats ambling about on what looked to be thin air against the dark cliffs on the left.

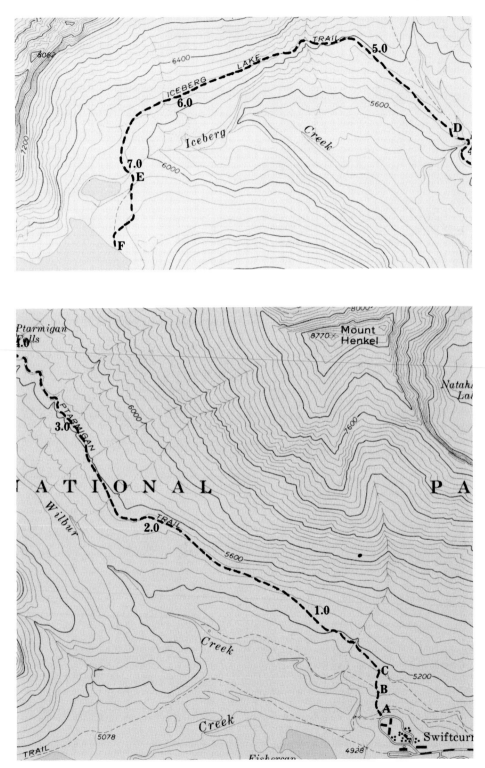

MOUNT BROWN LOOKOUT

Summary: The hike to Mount Brown Lookout involves one of the greatest elevation changes of any hike in Glacier Park. Starting from Sun Road across from Lake McDonald Lodge, it follows Gunsight Pass Trail up the north side of Snyder Creek to a junction. It then climbs steeply up the side of Mount Brown via Mount Brown Lookout Trail. Numerous switchbacks are involved. Views from the lookout are superb, and a mother mountain goat with two kids greeted us as we rounded the last bend--although we can't guarantee the mountain goats!

Length:
One way - 8.4 km
Round trip - 16.8 km
Dayhike
Season: Late June
Vehicle shuttle: No
Elevation extremes: 975-2279 m
Topographic maps:
Lake McDonald East
Mount Cannon

The trailhead is on the east side of Sun Road across from the road which exits the parking area at Lake McDonald Lodge. The exit road and the trailhead are located about 65 meters north of where Snyder Creek goes under Sun Road. The first part of this hike is along Gunsight Pass Trail which goes to Sperry Chalets. From the parking lot at Lake McDonald Lodge, it is possible--by craning the neck-- to spot Mount Brown lookout high above.

Although we have written about precautions in the introductory section of this book, some are especially applicable to this particular hike. The trail involves a considerable change in elevation, and long sections of it are steep. After leaving the Gunsight Pass Trail, there will be little or no water to drink unless it is carried along--as it should be because this trail can get to be hard, hot work. Get an early start, and be in shape.

The trail leaves Sun Road (A; 0.0) and, within 80 meters, passes the horse stables which are to the left of the trail. At 130 meters the trail passes to the right of a fenced treatment plant, and Snyder Creek thunders close by on the right.

The trail gradually climbs through a dense, mature forest of western red cedar and some western larch. Small hemlocks grow among the larger trees, and the forest floor is a thick, rich blanket of humus overlaid with mosses, ferns, queencup beadlilies, green bog-orchids and lush shrubs. Even the rocks and logs have a green veneer of moss. The sunshine filters down through the canopy or falls in long, bright shafts. The tree trunks and dead cottonwoods along Snyder Creek are vestiges of the 1964 Flood. As the trail steepens gradually and pulls away from the creek, the cedars gradually give way to Douglas fir and western white pine. Sometimes the large cones of the pine can be found along the trail.

At point B (2.8 km) there is a trail junction. Gunsight Pass Trail continues ahead to Sperry Chalets and Gunsight Pass. (For descriptions of hikes beyond point B, see "Snyder Lake," "Fish Lake" and "Gunsight Pass.") From the junction at point B, the Mount Brown Lookout Trail goes uphill to the left. It is narrower than Gunsight Pass Trail, and it is very steep from here on. Douglas fir and western white pine are found along the first section. Rocky Mountain maples and thinleaf alders occur as multiple-trunked shrubs, and huckleberry bushes and beargrass are common in the open forest. A red squirrel may chatter from the safety of a high branch. While you are not likely to spot one in the forest, the presence of elk is indicated by their droppings along the trail.

As the trail continues its climb, there is one particularly long series of switchbacks, only a few of which are indicated on the topographic map. As the altitude increases, subalpine fir and whitebark pine become the dominant trees, with subalpine fir growing almost to the lookout. There are a couple of long switchbacks just below the lookout which is at point

C (8.4 km) and trail's end.

The lookout perches on a rocky viewpoint that takes in a generous amount of scenery. Among the more prominent landmarks are Mount Brown (a little under 2 km distant), all of Lake McDonald, Heavens Peak, Stanton Mountain, the North Fork Valley and a number of peaks along the Continental Divide.

Look for mountain goats in the general vicinity of the lookout. If it is early in the season, they will look rather ratty and moth-eaten until their old coats are shed and the new growth comes in. Avoid close contact with them. Despite their quizzical expressions and chummy behavior, they are capable of inflicting serious injury if startled or cornered.

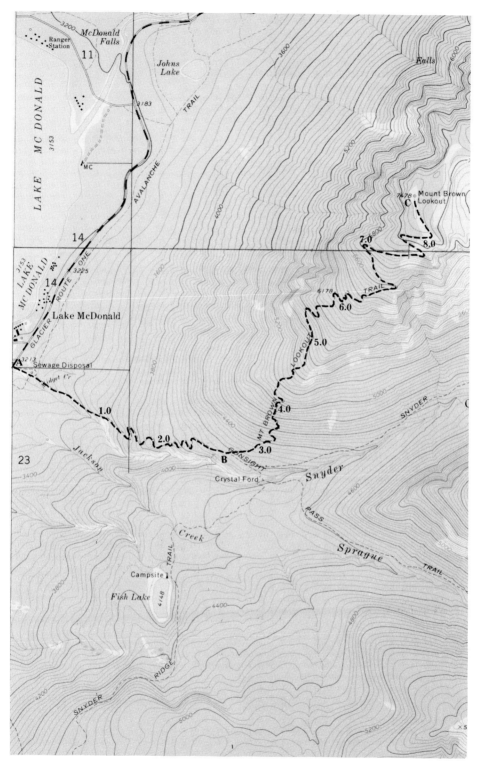

NORTH SHORE LAKE MC DONALD

Summary: Unlike most of Glacier's trails, this hike along Lake McDonald involves very little elevation change. Nonetheless, hikers should be well prepared before undertaking it. The hike starts from North Fork Road near Fish Creek Campground. The trail soon drops down to Fish Creek, then more or less parallels the shoreline of Lake McDonald. Despite the trail's nearness to the lake, the view is generally obscured by forest. The lake is bordered by a variety of forest types, the most interesting of which is a mature red cedar forest. The trail ends at the west end of North Lake McDonald Road.

Length:
    One way - 10.6 km
Dayhike
Season: Early June
Vehicle shuttle: Yes
Topographic map:
    Lake McDonald West

It is suggested that you make arrangements to have someone pick you up at the other end of this trail because it is long and ends at a little-used road where it is not easy to get a ride. (Some hikers make a long day of it and hike back the way they came.) To reach the trail's end by vehicle, take a road going west from Sun Road at the upper end of Lake McDonald. It is signed "McDonald Ranger Station." Continue past the ranger station to road's end.

The hike starts not far from the road entering Fish Creek Campground. From the campground entrance, continue north on North Fork Road for a short distance to a gravel pit on the left. The trailhead (A; 0.0) is on the right/east side of the road. Another part of this trail continues on the west side of the road and goes to the vicinity of Apgar, but it is not described here.

Because most of the trail is through dense forest which obscures the topographic features, please note that we do not indicate the kilometer marks on this particular map.

There is a dense lodgepole forest near the trailhead. Grasses, bracken fern, beargrass and snowberries grow along the edge of the trail as it drops downhill a short distance to Fish Creek. This fair-sized creek is the largest along this trail. Thinleaf alders are common along here, occasionally reaching the size of a small tree.

From the wooden bridge over Fish Creek, the trail climbs a short distance, then drops down to a trail junction at point **B (a little under 0.8 km)**. A trail comes in from the southeast loop of Fish Creek Campground, and North Shore Trail continues left. Bunchberries, with their distinctive four-petaled blossoms, are common along here. At point **C (a little over 0.8 km)** a short trail goes to the right to Rocky Point, a bluff overlooking Lake McDonald. The main route follows the left fork here. As the trail continues, there are some views of the west end of Lake McDonald and the Apgar area.

Howe Ridge Manway No. 1 (a seldom-used route) takes off on the left at point **D (1.1 km)**. As the trail continues, a few small western red cedars, Douglas firs and western hemlocks appear among the lodgepole pines. The trail comes down to the edge of Lake McDonald at a little under 3.0 km, the only place along the entire hike where it does so. There is a small rocky beach here, and there are good views of Mount Brown, Mount Cannon, Belton Mountain, Snyder Ridge, the Little Matterhorn and Edwards Mountain.

The entire route may best be described as gradually uphill and down, interspersed with many level stretches. At the 3.4-km point, the trail enters a well-defined forest of western red cedar, western white pine and western larch. Smaller hemlocks grow among the taller trees. This is a demarcation line between an old burn reforested by lodgepole pines and a mature forest which survived the fire. A few scarred stumps and snags indicate that the older forest did not escape the fire completely.

Many of the trees in this forest have relatively shallow root systems which spread out close to the surface. This is well illustrated at several points where the root systems of fallen trees are exposed. The density of the forest varies from one place to another. In some places it is thick and dark; in others it is open and park-like. Downed trees cover the ground in some areas; in others, the forest floor is deeply overlaid with the fallen needles of larch, pine and hemlock.

Several species of orchids grow along the North Shore Trail. Among these are striped coral-root, western coral-root, green bog-orchid and at least one of the species of twayblade orchids. We observed all of these on a single hike along this trail in June, and certainly we could have explored a little and found others. Some eighteen species of the orchid family have been reported for Glacier National Park. Mosses cover the logs and the ground in many places in the cedar forest, and there may be a lush growth of ferns, depending on the season. Look for Equisetum (or "horsetail") in wet areas.

The trail continues through the forest and ends at North Lake McDonald Road at point **E (10.6 km)**. From here it is 4.1 km (2.6 miles) via the road to the Lake McDonald Ranger Station and another 1.2 km (0.8 mile) from there to Sun Road.

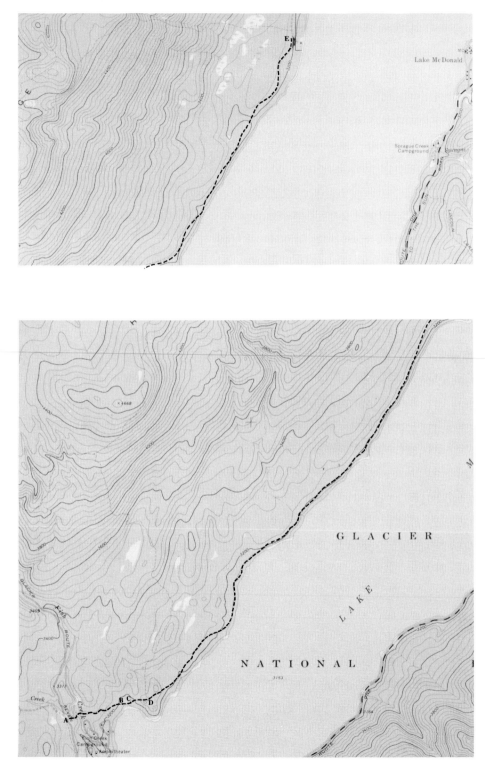

NUMA RIDGE LOOKOUT

Summary: From a trailhead near Bowman Lake Ranger Station, this hike follows Bowman Lake Trail along the lake, then climbs diagonally up Numa Ridge via Numa Ridge Lookout Trail. This lookout is somewhat isolated from much of the park's activities, but it is manned because of the great expanse of the park which can be seen from it.

Length:
  One way - 8.9 km
  Round trip - 17.8 km
Dayhike
Season: Early July
Vehicle shuttle: No
Elevation extremes: 1231-2121 m
Topographic maps:
  Quartz Ridge
  Kintla Peak

The trailhead is reached from Bowman Lake Campground. At the upper right/northeast side of the campground loop, a path goes off to the right to the ranger station which is a little over 100 meters away. The log ranger station/residence was originally a dining hall for the Skyland Boy's Camp which operated here in the 1920s. Continue past the left side of the building for an additional 60 meters to the trailhead (A; 0.0).

The route follows the Bowman Lake Trail from here. It proceeds above and a short distance back from the shoreline. There are some nice forest-framed views of the water from along this first stretch, with Rainbow Peak towering in the distance and Cerulean Ridge running along the far side of the lake. The forest is comprised of a variety of trees, including lodgepole pine, western larch, Engelmann spruce and Douglas fir.

There is a junction at point B (1.0 km) where Bowman Lake Trail continues ahead, eventually reaching Brown Pass and Goat Haunt Ranger Station some 34 km distant. Numa Ridge Lookout Trail heads left from this junction and diagonals up the wooded slopes of Numa Ridge.

A rather prominent feature that we noticed along this trail was the growth of many different kinds of shrubs and wildflowers--everything from wild rose and Rocky Mountain maple to blue penstemon and lodgepole pine. What looks like a homogenous area on the map proves to be one of unending variety on the ground. There are some mushy spots where the shrubbery grows riotously, and there are some open, park-like areas where the ground is thatched with pine needles and strewn with wildflowers.

The trail climbs steadily, although it occasionally flattens out for a short breather. The lodgepoles begin to drop out as Engelmann spruce, limber pines and subalpine firs begin to come in.

The trail ends at the lookout at point C (8.9 km). The elevation here is 2121 meters. The view seems endless and includes such landmarks as The Guardhouse, Mount Carter, Rainbow Peak, Square Peak, Vulture Peak, Logging Mountain, Cereulean and Quartz ridges, Bowman Lake, Akokala Lake, Reuter Peak and Numa Peak, in addition to many others. The dime-sized pond nestled in the woods below is known locally as "Moose Pond" (elevation 5035 on topo map), although it is doubtful whether any moose actually visit it. Rocky Mountain pond-lilies may be seen growing on it. The trail to the lookout actually passes quite close to it, but the pond is well camouflaged among the trees.

Food and drinking water are packed in to the lookout by mules, and water for washing is obtained from nearby snowbanks. Some lookout personnel return year after year, others find one season of solitude is enough. Some of the lookouts which were manned regularly in the past are now occupied only during periods of high fire danger, if at all.

Animal life in the area surrounding the lookout includes pikas, golden-mantled ground squirrels and Clark's nutcrackers. An occasional deer, elk or bear is sighted from here.

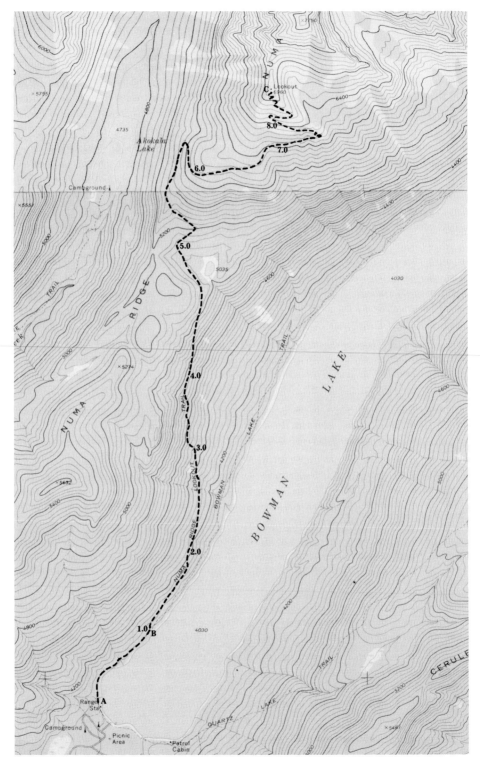

OLDMAN LAKE

Summary: The hike to Oldman Lake starts near Two Medicine Campground and follows Pitamakin Pass Trail along the base of Rising Wolf Mountain and then up Dry Fork Valley. After climbing through the open landscape of the old Dry Fork Burn, the trail enters a forest of limber pines and soon ends at Oldman Lake.

Length:
  One way - 10.2 km
  Round trip - 20.4 km
Dayhike or overnight
Season: Mid June
Vehicle shuttle: No
Elevation extremes: 1574-2026 m
Topographic maps:
  Squaw Mountain
  Kiowa
  Cut Bank Pass

From Two Medicine Campground the trailhead is reached by crossing the bridge below the outlet of Pray Lake. (Pray Lake is the small lake just to the west of the campground, and the bridge is easily seen from the road.) The distance from the road to the trailhead across the bridge is about 140 meters. Here there is a "T" in the trail. The trail going left is Dawson Pass Trail (see "Upper Two Medicine Lake"). The trail to Oldman Lake starts (A; 0.0) by going to the right on the Pitamakin Pass Trail.

The trail climbs along the base of Rising Wolf Mountain, shaded by Douglas firs and Engelmann spruce. There are some interesting views of Two Medicine Creek winding through the willows below, and Scenic Point and Appistoki Peak can be seen from at least one point along this first part of the hike. Among the things we saw were lots of wildflowers and fat, querulous robins. The trail turns up the Dry Fork Valley, still following along the base of Rising Wolf. At 2.1 km there is a series of falls coming down the side of the mountain, although they may fade as the season advances. The trail drops down to the valley floor at 2.7 km, then proceeds through a patchy

landscape of forests and clearings below the talus slopes and cliffs of Rising Wolf.

The trail crosses to the right/north side of the Dry Fork at point B (3.5 km). It then leaves the creek bottom and heads north up a rocky drainage to a junction at point C (3.8 km) where the Dry Fork Trail goes to the right/southeast to the Two Medicine entrance station area. Pitamakin Pass Trail goes to the left/west and continues up the valley. (Because of its location at the edge of a drainage subject to flooding, it is possible that the exact location of this junction could change in the future.) The trail climbs steadily along the slopes of the drainage. Red Mountain is on the right/north of the trail.

Between the junction at point C and the lake, there are some areas dominated by lodgepole pine and other areas where limber pine and subalpine fir are dominant. As the trail continues to climb, it passes an un-named lake (elevation 6182 feet on the topo map) which sits in a cirque on the side of Rising Wolf. Although the water cannot be seen, the depression containing the lake is visible from the trail.

Between the 6- and 7-km points, the trail crosses a large, open area created by the Dry Fork Burn which swept through the valley in 1929. Common juniper and buffaloberry grow here, and the wind often sings through the brush and creaking snags. There are fine views of Flinsch Peak and Mount Morgan from along here. (Oldman Lake lies in a cirque below Mount Morgan.)

There is a trail junction at point D (9.2 km) where Pitamakin Pass Trail goes to the right (see "Pitamakin Pass"). The hike described here follows the left fork into an open forest of limber pines.

The forest path comes out at Oldman Lake at point E (10.2 km). Some large cutthroat trout inhabit this fair-sized lake, but they are wiley, well fed, and not easily taken in. The far side of the lake abuts the steep slopes of Mount Morgan. Now and then, hikers can be spotted as they toil up the switchbacks to Pitamakin Pass above the lake.

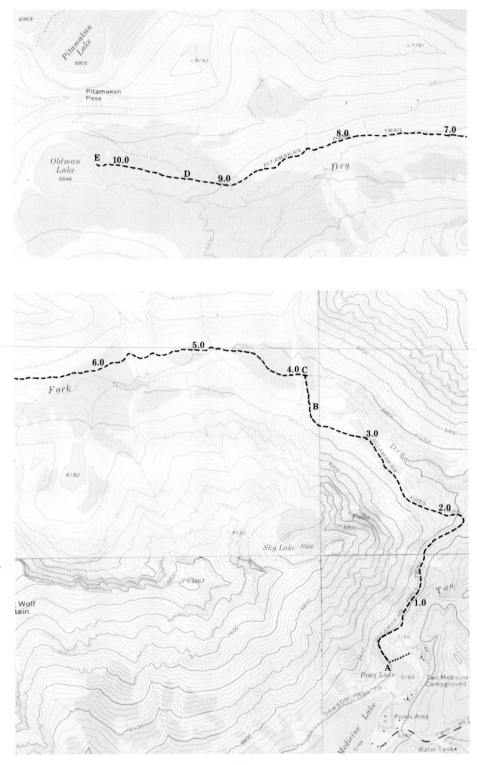

OTOKOMI LAKE

Summary: From the vicinity of Rising Sun, Rose Creek Trail climbs to Otokomi Lake through forest above and somewhat parallel to Rose Creek. The lake lies in a glacial amphitheater and is bordered by steep, gray cliffs and subalpine meadows. There are several waterfalls near the lake.

Length:
  One way - 8.5 km
  Round trip - 17.0 km
Dayhike or overnight
Season: Mid June
Vehicle shuttle: No
Elevation extremes: 1414-1976 m
Topographic map:
  Rising Sun

The somewhat obscure trailhead is in the vicinity of Rising Sun Motor Inn on the east side of the park. From the general store, hike up the paved road on the right/east side of the building. Continue for about 275 meters, passing through the cabin area. The trail takes off (A; 0.0) from the upper paved loop. The last time we made this hike, the trailhead sign was located a short distance in along the trail.

The trail swings close to Rose Creek, then climbs. Douglas fir, Rocky Mountain maple, mountain ash and thimbleberry grow in this area. The route soon makes several switchbacks as it continues to climb. Lodgepole pines become the dominant trees, with smaller Douglas firs coming up among them.

Like most of Glacier's trails, Rose Creek Trail has its share of wildflowers. The species in bloom vary with the seasons and the years. Some of the flowers to be found along this trail include Indian-paintbrush (at least eight species have been reported for the park), mariposa lily, beargrass, meadowrue, wild rose, spotted coralroot, lupine, silky phacelia, elephant-head and blue clematis. There are periodic views of Rose Creek Gorge which is deep and very impressive in places. The dark green pools below some of the drops look enticing, but there is tremendous power in the currents and eddies that may not be visible on the surface. Every few years, drownings occur when people fall into these rough-and-tumble creeks or attempt to swim in the pools. The best of swimmers may prove to be no match for the force and numbing cold of the water.

At about 2.4 km there are fine views of Goat Mountain which is nearby and Red Eagle, Mahtotopa, Little Chief and Citadel mountains which are on the far side of St. Mary Lake to the south.

As the trail continues its climb, it passes through some relatively open areas dominated by shrubs such as cow-parsnip and thinleaf alder. Grizzlies are partial to areas such as these, so be alert. Farther up the trail, Engelmann spruce appear; and nearer the lake, these tend to give way to subalpine firs and limber pines. Common juniper grows in mats at the bases of the trees, many of which have been twisted into unusual shapes by the wind. The trail crosses some scree slopes from which there are superb backward views toward Divide Peak in the far distance.

After crossing the screes, the trail drops down through subalpine firs and meadows spangled with yellow buttercups to Rose Creek. It then follows the creek upstream a short distance to Otokomi Lake at point B (8.5 km). This little cirque lake is hemmed in snugly by the sheer cliffs forming three sides of Rose Basin. The creek and basin were named after Charles Rose, an explorer whose Indian name, "Otokomi," meant "Yellow Fish." The name was misspelled "Roes" by early cartographers, which accounts for the different spelling on the maps.

Steep scree slopes plunge to the shoreline, and some patches of snow may survive well into the summer.

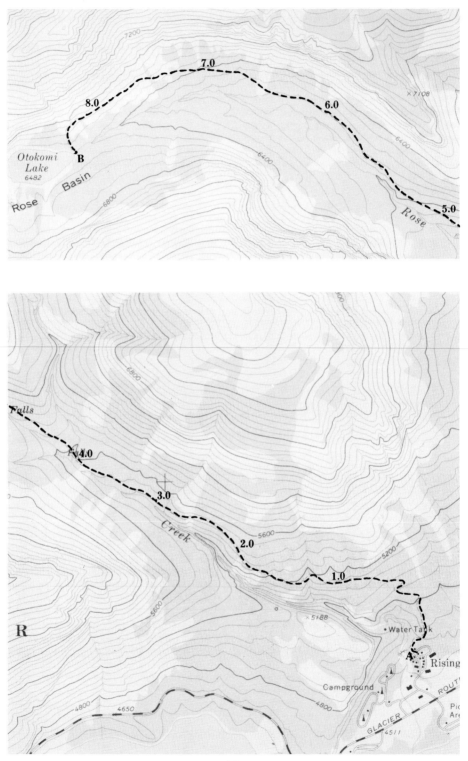

PITAMAKIN PASS

Summary: Pitamakin Pass Trail starts near Cut Bank Campground, follows the North Fork Cut Bank Creek in a southwesterly direction, then heads south. It passes near several lakes, including Morning Star and Katoya, climbs to Pitamakin Pass, then drops down near Oldman Lake. From there it goes down the Dry Fork before winding around the base of Rising Wolf Mountain and ending a short distance from Two Medicine Campground.

Length:
   One way - 28.0 km
Dayhike or overnight
Season: Mid July
Vehicle shuttle: Yes
Elevation extremes: 1582-2322 m
Topographic maps:
   Cut Bank Pass
   Kiowa
   Squaw Mountain

This trailhead is on the righthand side of the road as you enter Cut Bank Campground. The campground is reached by taking a signed, graded road west from U.S. 89 between the towns of St. Mary and East Glacier.

The trail starts (A; 0.0) as a two-track road which crosses a grassy meadow inhabited by Columbian ground squirrels and visited by butterflies and bees. Rufous-tailed chipmunks flirt around the forested campground area. At about 0.4 km the two-track road swings off to the left, and this hike continues along the trail which goes to the right. It trends gradually uphill a short distance from the willow thickets bordering North Fork Cut Bank Creek. Be warned that the Cut Bank Valley is notorious for its man-eating mosquitoes, so have the repellent handy. The area is forested with Douglas fir, spruce and some patches of lodgepole pine, occasionally fading into open areas. Mad Wolf and Bad Marriage mountains can be seen to the south of the trail. At 2.7 km Kupunkamint Mountain is to the north of the trail.

At point B (3.7 km) the trail crosses a wide, rocky creek bed. This creek (perhaps dry) drains the valley between the two mountains, Kupunkamint and Amphitheater. Black cottonwoods grow a short distance downstream from the crossing.

Red squirrels are particularly common along the first section of this trail, as indicated by piles of cone scales at the bases of trees or heaped on logs. Approaching hikers often trigger incessant chattering and acrobatics in the trees near the trail.

There is a trail junction at point C (6.2 km). The righthand fork is Triple Divide Pass Trail which goes to Medicine Grizzly Lake and Triple Divide Pass. Red Eagle Lake can also be reached by taking the righthand fork. The hike we describe here continues on Pitamakin Pass Trail (shown as Cut Bank Pass Trail on the topo map) which is the lefthand fork.

As it heads south, the trail crosses Atlantic Creek at point D (6.6 km) just below Atlantic Falls. The creek drains Medicine Grizzly Lake, cascading over small ledges and creating a low, resonant falls. From here the trail heads uphill, following above and to the west of North Fork Cut Bank Creek. Medicine Grizzly Peak is on the west side of the trail. The route crosses some big open slopes giving onto grassy meadows embroidered with wildflowers. Eagle Plume and Red mountains loom above the valley to the east.

A grizzly had also been active in this area. Sod was torn up in the meadows, and there were fresh droppings on the trail. We made a lot of noise as we hiked through here, although our first instincts were to sneak through on tiptoe! As the trail continues, it passes through alternate areas of forest and open slopes. It crosses the outlet of Morning Star Lake at point E (10.6 km). We try not to describe lakes as "gems," but this one really is a gem, set among grassy slopes and scattered copses of dark subalpine firs. If the wind is not blowing, the shallow, greenish waters beautifully reflect the highcountry scenery. The trail passes a short distance to the east of the lake.

At about the 11-km point, the trail begins to climb more steeply, and subalpine firs become increasingly common. Many of these show the "flag" effect created by prevailing winds, the branches tending to be concentrated on the downwind side of the trees. The steep switchbacks continue to about the 12-km point, although there are additional steep areas ahead. At point **F (12.2 km)** the trail crosses a small creek which drains Katoya Lake. It then climbs steeply, and Katoya Lake can be seen from the switchbacks.

In July, pasque flowers and glacier-lilies are often abundant in these meadows. The trail becomes more gradual in its ascent as it approaches Pitamakin Lake. It crosses the outlet of the lake at point **G (13.7 km)**. Talus slopes, snowbanks and sheer cliffs border the south end of the lake, and Pitamakin Pass looms high above. Mount Morgan and McClintock Peak can be seen from here.

After leaving Pitamakin Lake, the going is uphill again. Look for white-crowned sparrows and chipping sparrows in this area. The trail climbs toward Pitamakin Pass via a series of steep switchbacks, passing above the murky, aqua waters of Lake of the Seven Winds.

Most of the plants growing in the area show adaptations to the severe environmental conditions (strong winds, shallow soil, short growing season, extreme cold, etc.). Subalpine fir and spruce grow in mats. Moss campion and alpine forget-me-nots hug the ground, and there were a number of other wildflowers here with which we weren't familiar.

Pitamakin Pass is at point **H (15.7 km)**. We were met in the pass by two hoary marmots, the wind ruffling their fur and tugging at our packs. It was getting late in the day, and the shadows were lengthening in the valley behind while the pass still glowed in the sun. There is a trail junction here where Dawson Pass Trail goes to the west, and the Pitamakin Pass Trail continues east along the ridge. Some hikers may prefer to avoid the vehicle shuttle by returning from here to Cut Bank Campground via the route just taken.

At point **I (16.0 km)** Pitamakin Pass Trail swings to the right and switchbacks downhill toward Oldman Lake. The switchbacks end at point **J (17.6 km)**, and the trail soon enters an open forest of large limber pines. It continues to a junction at point **K (18.8 km)** where a trail goes right/west to Oldman Lake (see "Oldman Lake"). From the junction, the main trail continues east, where it enters the area of the old Dry Fork Burn at 19.1 km. Numerous snags are a bleak reminder of the fire that swept through the valley in 1929. As the trail continues downhill, it is north of the Dry Fork and somewhat parallel to it. There are intermittent stands of trees along the trail as it crosses the relatively dry slopes, and lodgepole pines gradually become the dominant tree.

The trail crosses a wide, rocky drainage at point **L (24.1 km)**; watch for cairns marking the route here. There is a trail junction on the east side of this drainage at point **M (24.2 km)**. The exact location of this junction may be subject to change, being situated in an area susceptible to flooding. The left fork is the Dry Fork Trail which goes over to Two Medicine Road. The main trail described here continues down the rocky drainage and crosses Dry Fork at point **N (24.5 km)**. Later in the season, this creek has a tendency to live up to its name.

After crossing the creek, the trail bends around the base of Rising Wolf Mountain. It enters a forest of lodgepole, spruce and fir as it swings around above Two Medicine Creek. There are views of Lower Two Medicine Lake and Scenic Point from a few spots along the trail. The trail ends at a junction with Dawson Pass Trail (see "Upper Two Medicine") at point **O (28.0 km)**. From the junction, a short trail goes left, crosses a bridge and comes out at Two Medicine Campground.

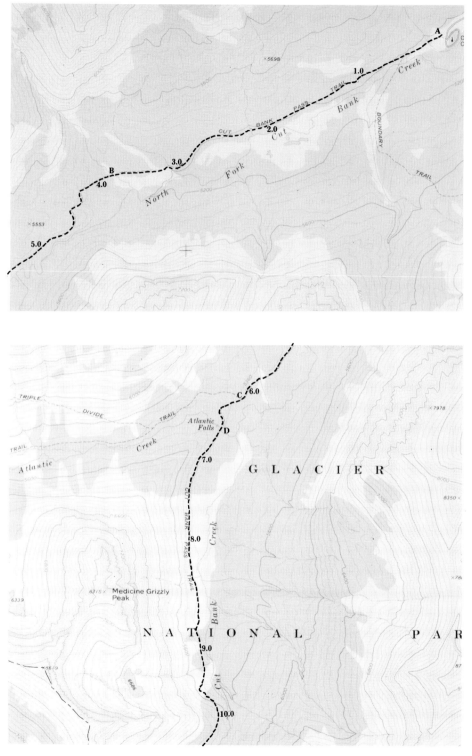

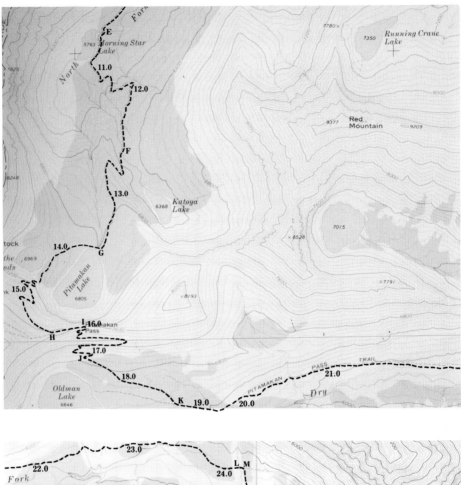

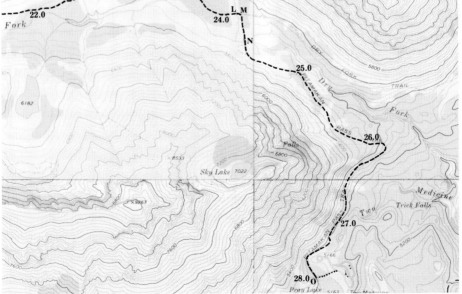

QUARTZ LAKE LOOP

Summary: From a trailhead near Bowman Lake Campground, the trail skirts the end of the lake, then climbs diagonally up and over Cerulean Ridge. It then drops down to the edge of Quartz Lake before passing between Quartz Lake and Middle Quartz Lake. It then heads west, not far from the south shore of Middle Quartz. It soon travels along Lower Quartz, crosses its outlet and climbs over Quartz Ridge. From the top of the ridge, the route drops down to Bowman Lake, and the loop is completed back at the trailhead.

Length:
    Round trip - 21.1 km
Dayhike or overnight
Season: Mid June
Vehicle shuttle: No
Elevation extremes: 1228-1682 m
Topographic map:
    Quartz Ridge

This hike starts near the boat ramp adjacent to Bowman Lake Campground. (This ramp is just to the right as you enter the big campground loop.) As you face Bowman Lake, the trail starts (A; 0.0) by heading right/southeast. It crosses the outlet of the lake at point B (0.3 km) where a wooden bridge spans Bowman Creek. Thinleaf alder and red-osier dogwood grow as shrubs along the banks of the creek.

After crossing Bowman Creek, the trail wanders close to the shoreline for a short distance, providing some excellent views of the big lake which sits in a glacier-carved valley. At about 0.5 km the trail leaves the shoreline and soon passes a patrol cabin. It is occupied by park personnel during the summer season and used by rangers out on patrol in the winter. Snowshoes are sometimes used to gain access to these remote areas in the winter, but rangers usually use cross-country skis. Engelmann spruce and western larch are the common conifers here.

Not far beyond the cabin, the trail begins to climb. There is a trail junction at point C (a little under 1.0 km) where the right fork goes to Lower Quartz Lake. Hikers following the hike described here will eventually return on this trail to complete a loop. The hike as we describe it begins the loop by taking the left fork which heads steadily up Cerulean Ridge. Spruce, firs and larches grow along here. In general, the hike is through forest except for an occasional open area. Mosses and dog-toothed lichens grow in moist areas, and only the most resolute hiker will be able to march by the thimbleberries, huckleberries and wild strawberries if they are ripe. Foamflower, meadowrue and large-leaved avens are among the many flowers along the trail.

Between the 4- and 5-km points, the trail becomes less steep as it crosses the flatter part of Cerulean Ridge. It continues across the top to point D (7.3 km). It then diagonals down the other side of Cerulean Ridge, providing some glimpses of all three of the Quartz lakes. Lodgepole pines are the common tree along this south-facing slope.

The trail drops down to the west end of Quartz Lake (there is no "Upper Quartz Lake") at point E (10.2 km), and a short hike over to the lake reveals a pretty little beach of smooth pebbles. Like the other two Quartz lakes, forest slopes down to the lake's edge on all sides. This is a picturesque spot with the best views of the trip. Instead of making the loop hike which is described here, many hikers make this their destination and return the way they came. Depending on the season, the route ahead may cross some mushy spots where brush crowds the trail and mosquitoes may be particularly bothersome.

From point E, the trail continues ahead/south, passing between Quartz Lake and Middle Quartz Lake. At a trail fork at point F (10.3 km), the left fork goes a short distance to a log patrol cabin near the lakeshore. The hike follows the right fork at point F and soon crosses Quartz Creek via a bridge at point G (10.7 km). As the trail continues, it passes to the left/south of Middle Quartz Lake. Bridges cross some of the mushy areas along here, and parts of the trail may be obscured due to the lush growth.

The trail does not swing over to the Middle Quartz shoreline. As it continues in a southwesterly direction, there are some ups and downs along the route. Quartz Lake can soon be glimpsed through the forest below. The trail proceeds above this lake for its entire length. On Quartz Ridge (opposite the lake) a number of dead lodgepole pines can be seen--the destructive work of the mountain pine beetle. In 1977 the beetles reached almost epidemic proportions here, and while hiking the short distance from the head of Lower Quartz to its foot, we heard three pines crash to the ground on the ridge. The larval stages do the most damage. These beetle infestations reach major proportions in a cyclical fashion, and the infestation in the North Fork is considered to be a natural phenomenon. The infestation will eventually die out and re-occur at some future time.

There is another junction at point **H (a little over 15.0 km)**. The left fork is the Quartz Creek Trail which continues to the North Fork Road. (That trail may be overgrown in some areas.) The route described here follows the righthand fork, heads down and crosses the outlet of Lower Quartz Lake at point **I (15.1 km)**. The creek is 33 meters wide and shallow in most spots. From the bridge, the trail enters a fir-larch forest and leaves the lake, climbing steadily up the side of Quartz Ridge. It passes through several moist areas where green bog orchids grow. Lodgepole pines are also common.

The trail tops out on Quartz Ridge at point **J (17.8 km)**. It then continues through the forest, heading diagonally downhill. There are some switchbacks along this stretch. The loop is completed back at point C **(20.1 km)**. From here the trail described earlier goes left to the trailhead at point **A (21.1 km)** beside Bowman Lake.

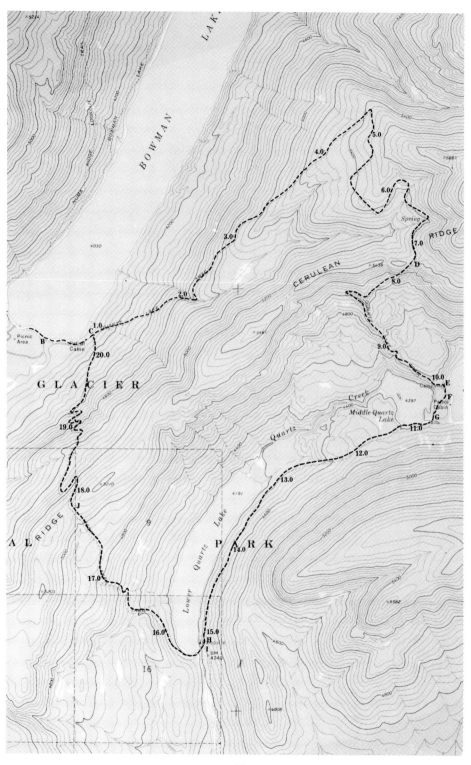

RED EAGLE LAKE

Summary: The hike to Red Eagle Lake is partly over an old, closed-off road and partly over trail. Most of the route is through forest, with some ups and downs but no major elevation changes. Red Eagle Creek is crossed twice via suspension bridges. (If travelling early or late in the season, make inquiry to be sure the bridges are installed.) The destination is a good-sized lake in a picturesque setting.

Length:
    One way - 12.9 km including old road
    Round trip - 25.8 km
Dayhike or overnight
Season: Mid June
Vehicle shuttle: No
Elevation extremes: 1372 - 1463 m
Topographic maps:
    Saint Mary
    Rising Sun

From U.S. 89 in the town of St. Mary, proceed 0.2 mile to the park entrance. Continue toward the St. Mary visitor center for an additional 0.1 mile, then turn left toward the St. Mary Ranger Station, and proceed 0.7 mile on this road to a junction where the road to the present ranger station goes to the left. The road to the trailhead continues for 0.2 mile to the parking area below the old 1913 ranger station at point X.

The hike begins by following the old road that continues beyond the parking area for 6.5 km to point A where it becomes a trail. There is a meadow on the righthand side of the road and forest on the left. At. 0.6 km there is a road fork; the route to Red Eagle Lake follows the lefthand fork. The road continues, passing through á Douglas fir-Engelmann spruce forest interspersed with many grassy meadows decked out in the latest wildflowers and bordered by stands of aspen.

From about the 3.7-km point along the road, a large, open meadow affords good views of the surrounding mountains--Divide, Curly Bear, Triple Divide Peak, Red Eagle, Mahtotopa, Little

Chief, Citadel, Fusillade, Goat, Otokomi, East Flattop and Singleshot. The old St. Mary Lake fire lookout can also be seen. Among the wildflowers on the sunny meadows, look for wild hollyhocks, sticky geraniums, wild roses, thistles and salsify.

Unless it has been repaired, there is a road washout at 5.8 km. (This is mentioned to give you some idea of your location along the road.) The hike thus far may best be described as a gradual climb with many level areas and some ups and downs. There are no great elevation changes. The road fizzles out at the far end of a meadow at 6.5 km. There is a good view of Triple Divide Peak far ahead, and the meadow is lumpy with pocket gopher mounds.

The trail starts from here (A; 0.0), and trail distances are calculated from this point where the road becomes a bonafide trail. Dropping downhill, the trail soon enters a forest which is broken by occasional open areas. At point B (0.6 km) a suspension bridge crosses Red Eagle Creek--location approximate on map. These bridges have been built in the last few years, successors of the traditional log bridges which would wash out periodically. Heed the warning that limits one hiker to the bridge at a time, and don't be tempted to bounce or get a bridge to swinging; it could break and cause serious injury. Alders grow along this stream, as do black cottonwoods with their deeply-furrowed, gray bark. The trail continues to a junction at point C (1.1 km)--location approximate on map. The righthand fork is the seldom-used St. Mary Lake Trail which heads toward that lake and eventually passes Virginia Falls. The left fork is the trail to Red Eagle Lake. Red Eagle Creek is re-crossed via a second suspension bridge at point D (1.2 km)--location approximate on map. The trail continues in the vicinity of Red Eagle Creek, climbing several bluffs as it works its way upstream.

Fireweed, meadowrue, cow-parsnip, elderberry and shrub willow grow in some of the more open areas while queencup beadlily, whortleberry, arnica and northern twinflower are common on the more shaded forest floor.

At point **E (just under 6.0 km)** the trail crosses a fair-sized, rocky creek bottom. Not far beyond here, it climbs steeply up a forested glacial moraine. Just beyond the top of this moraine is a trail fork at point **F (6.3 km)**. The left fork is the Triple Divide Trail which continues to the head of the lake and eventually climbs to Triple Divide Pass. The righthand fork drops down to Red Eagle Lake at point **G (6.4 km)**.

The slopes of Red Eagle Mountain come down to the right/west side of the lake while those of Kakitos Mountain border the left/east shore. This is a good-sized lake bordered partly by spruce-fir forest and partly by open terrain. The outlet is to the right of point G. A sizeable rainbow trout or cutthroat trout may occasionally be caught in the lake.

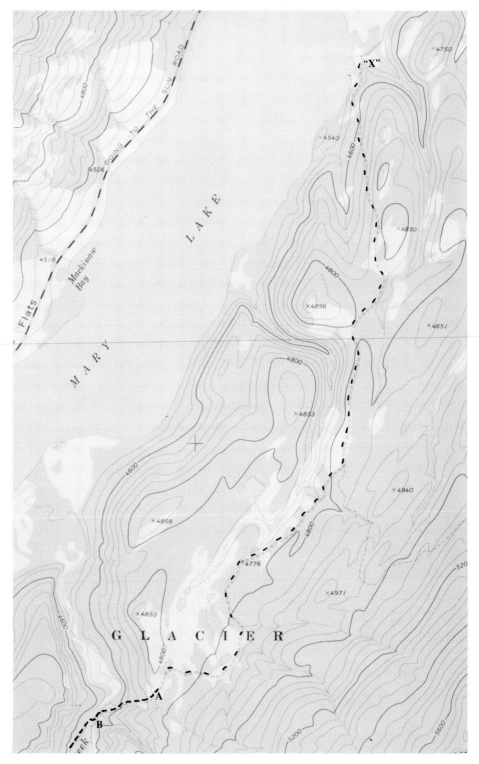

SCENIC POINT

Summary: This hike follows Mount Henry Trail from Two Medicine Road to Scenic Point. It climbs gradually at first, then more steeply to an alpine area near Scenic Point. The climb is long and arduous. There are many interesting wildflowers along the trail, and--as the elevation increases--the views are increasingly panoramic. From the vicinity of Scenic Point, hikers may return via the same route or continue to the town of East Glacier; however, this description ends at Scenic Point.

Length:
    One way - 6.0 km
    Round trip - 12.0 km
Dayhike
Season: Mid June
Vehicle shuttle: No
Elevation extremes: 1606-2252 m
Topographic maps:
    Squaw Mountain
    East Glacier Park

The trailhead is reached by hiking east from the ranger station on Two Medicine Road for a little over 400 meters. A short spur road goes off to the right/southeast here. The trail starts (A; 0.0) about 15 meters in on the lefthand side of this spur road and follows the Mount Henry Trail. Both Appistoki Peak and Scenic Point are visible from Two Medicine Road.

Trees near the trailhead include subalpine fir, Douglas fir, Engelmann spruce and lodgepole pine. After passing through this forest for about 0.5 km, the route crosses an area where young pines and firs are coming up among a litter of dead snags. The trail soon approaches Appistoki Creek where the effects of floods in 1964 and 1975 are still apparent. The landscape in places has been scoured and overlaid with tons of rocks and gravel and logs.

The trail continues from here to a junction at point B (0.9 km) where a short side trail goes 70 meters to an overlook from which there is a fine view of Appistoki Falls. Heed the warning signs and do not leave the trail--the area is potentially dangerous, and a slip could be fatal.

From the junction at point B, the Mount Henry Trail goes uphill to the left. It climbs steadily and soon begins a series of switchbacks. (While these switchbacks are represented on the topo map, there are many more than the map indicates.) As it continues to climb, the trail passes above Appistoki Falls. The trees become fewer in number, generally smaller, and they show the effects of strong winds and heavy snows. Common juniper grows in mats along these slopes. Another hardy shrub in the area is the russet buffaloberry. Its leaves are dark green above with numerous brown spots beneath.

The highcountry through which the trail climbs toward Scenic Point is an excellent example of subalpine and alpine conditions in the park. Golden-mantled ground squirrels whisk in and out among the rocks and gnarled tree roots. Appistoki Creek becomes an increasingly thin ribbon far below. There are also views of Two Medicine Lake and the nearby beaver ponds, Paradise Point, Pray Lake and a portion of Upper Two Medicine Lake. Appistoki, Sinopah, Lone Walker and Rising Wolf are among the peaks visible along the climb.

Trees are eventually left behind as the trail continues to ascend. The area is rocky, and there are switchbacks up the talus slopes. (Again, there are more switchbacks than the map indicates.) Do not cut across switchbacks as this will greatly contribute to erosion problems.

The trail tops out at point C (a little under 5.0 km). This is the end of the steep climb. From here the route is along the left/northeast side of Point 7277. (The original topo map shows it going along the right/southwest side of this point.) There are steep talus slopes along the trail, and care should be taken not to slip. A reminder--Glacier's trails should not be traversed until park crews have been over them, although they are not officially closed unless posted. Each season, ranger personnel receive current lists of the trails as they are checked out, and you should contact a ranger before planning any hike. A slip on a snowbank could result in a fatal slide. (We often carry an ice axe, even on cleared trails if there is a possibility of snowbanks or ice.) There is also the possibility of plunging through a thin crust of snow into a hole below.

From the end of the steep climb at point C, the trail ascends more gradually. Scenic Point is visible ahead, and the view encompasses many prominent landmarks. Two Medicine Creek forms an oxbow far below; Dry Fork Valley, which leads to Oldman Lake, can be seen in the distance; Red Mountain and Spot Mountain are among the mountains in the scenery.

At point **D (5.3 km)** the trail swings out onto an open part of the mountain. The Blackfeet Reservation stretches out into the distance. No trees grow here, but the dry, rocky terrain may be a patchwork of wildflowers, the variety changing as the season progresses. One of our favorites--carpet pink, or moss campion--forms small, dense mats among the rocks. Many of the rocks have lichens on them. These are a pioneer species of plant, growing on bare rock where few other plants can survive. Each plant consists of two different organisms, an alga and a fungus. In identifying and classifying lichens, botanists consider not only their growth form and color but the manner in which they react with various chemical reagents. Most of the lichens in this area are black.

At point **E (6.0 km)** the trail has reached the Scenic Point area and soon begins the long descent towards East Glacier. This makes a good point to turn around.

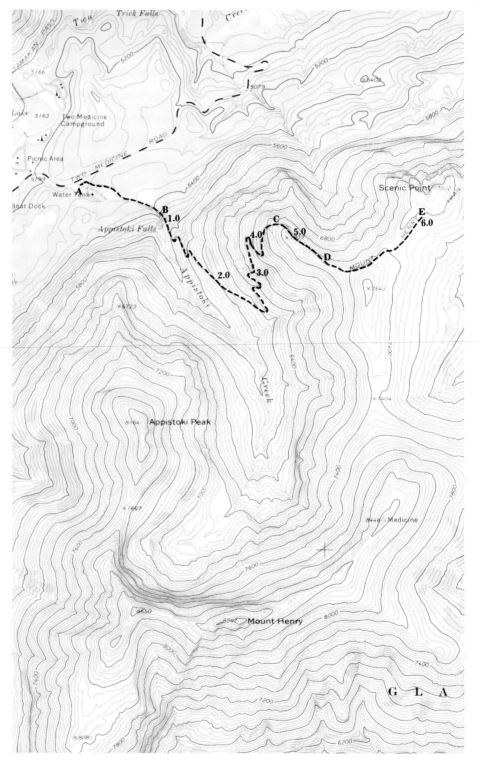

SIYEH PASS

Summary: This hike is over parts of three trails--Siyeh Bend Cut-off Trail, Piegan Pass Trail and Siyeh Pass Trail. From a trailhead at Siyeh Bend along Sun Road, the hike proceeds first through a forest, then through a more open landscape of meadows, subalpine larches and firs. It then climbs the relatively barren talus slopes to a high point near Siyeh Pass. From the high point, it descends steeply via a long series of switchbacks, passing a side trail to nearby Sexton Glacier. Upon reaching the area of Baring Creek, it proceeds in the general vicinity of the creek down to Sun Road.

Length:
  One way - 16.4 km
Dayhike
Season: Mid July
Vehicle shuttle: Yes
Elevation extremes: 1424-2484 m
Topographic maps:
  Logan Pass
  Rising Sun

The first part of this hike follows the Siyeh Bend Cut-off Trail. The trailhead (A; 0.0) is east of Logan Pass at Siyeh Bend where Siyeh Creek flows under Sun Road. From the road, the trail immediately heads down toward the edge of the creek, then climbs along its right/east side. Siyeh Creek is very interesting along here. The water runs down through an area where the rock strata are tilted, and the creek passes completely under some overhanging ledges in places.

The trail soon leaves Siyeh Creek, switching back and to the right. Subalpine firs and small spruce grow here. The route soon enters an area of good-sized spruce and fir. Vegetation along here tends to be fairly dense and includes willows, alders, cow-parsnip, menziesia, elderberry, meadowrue and huckleberry. The distinctive call of the varied thrush, a relative of the robin, can often be heard. The male has a reddish-brown breast with a dark band across it.

The trail continues to climb through the forest, diagonalling along the slopes to about 1.6 km. It then drops down for a short distance, crossing several small creeks before it again climbs to a junction at point B (1.9 km). From here the hike follows Piegan Pass Trail which is the lefthand fork. The route is partly through open, grassy meadows and partly through forest. Signs of grizzly activity were much in evidence the last time we made this hike--fresh droppings on the trail and some plowed-up meadows. As the trail continues, there are rewarding views of Going-to-the-Sun Mountain and Matahpi Peak. Sexton Glacier lies on the opposite/east side of the saddle connecting these two peaks, and there will be some nice views of it coming up.

There is an avalanche area at 2.7 km, and wildflowers are often abundant after the snows melt. Siyeh Creek is crossed at point C (3.8 km) via a small log bridge. From a junction at point D (4.1 km) the left fork is Piegan Pass Trail which continues to Morning Eagle Falls and the Many Glacier area. The hike described here now follows Siyeh Pass Trail which is the righthand fork. It passes through Preston Park, a landscape of subalpine firs scattered over windswept meadows. The grade is gradually uphill for the most part.

Subalpine larches begin to appear along the trail at 4.6 km. The subalpine larch is one of the park's most unusual trees, being--unofficially, at least--the Park Tree. It is found in a few scattered locations about the park, growing at high elevations and reaching full tree size in areas too harsh for other trees to achieve height. Unlike most other conifers, the larch has deciduous needles that are shed in the fall.

After leaving the Preston Park area, the trail begins to climb more steadily as it works its way up the talus slopes. As it continues to climb, there are several series of switchbacks. These long climbs at high elevations require pacing, which isn't too difficult with some of the park's loftiest scenery to admire. Two small, un-named lakes can be seen from the trail as it gains altitude. Moss campion and alpine forget-me-nots grow along these relatively barren slopes.

While writing this manuscript during the winter, our notes bring back many memories of Glacier's trails. Our favorite haunts prove to have been in the barren, wind-scoured highcountry-- Siyeh Pass, Pitamakin Pass, Swiftcurrent Lookout and Scenic Point. The plants and animals are specially adapted for survival in the harsh environment, although the highcountry ecology is extremely fragile. Please be especially careful to stay on the trail. Don't cut switchbacks or do anything else which could upset the delicate scheme of things.

The trail ends its grinding climb at 7.4 km. There is a superb view of Boulder Creek drainage as the trail swings around to the right, and there may be mountain goats among the cliffs in the area. The trail soon drops down slightly to a cairn at point **E (7.6 km)**. Note that Siyeh Pass is actually a short distance north of the switchbacks which ascended to this point; it is a broad, obvious saddle.

This might be a good point to reinforce our introductory material on Glacier's quixotic weather. We started this hike in clouds at Siyeh Bend, but they soon cleared and the weather was sunny through Preston Park. Part way up to the pass, the rain began, and an electrical storm was nipping at our heels as we descended rapidly from the area of the pass. The rain turned to snow as we left the top, and this turned to rain and hail farther down. Then--for the last couple of kilometers--the sun came out enough to dry us off. But it was raining again by the time we reached Sun Road!

From point E, the trail soon drops steeply via a long, arduous series of switchbacks. The barren contours gradually soften as vegetation increases. There are excellent views of Sexton Glacier, Baring Creek and part of St. Mary Lake far below.

A side trail to the glacier leaves the main trail at point **F (9.0 km)**, but stay off the glacier itself as there may be crevasses concealed beneath a thin crust of ice or snow. Siyeh Pass Trail continues on the left.

From point F, the trail continues its descent via the switchbacks to about 11.4 km. It more or less parallels Baring Creek, but from a fair distance, as it descends along the slopes. Goat Mountain is off to the left. The country is relatively open in places, interspersed with subalpine firs and shrubs.

Baring Creek is very pretty as it races down over the mudstone. The trail enters a mature forest of Engelmann spruce, lodgepole pine and Douglas fir at 15.3 km. The creek can be heard from the trail but is not generally visible. There are places where a short side trip will afford some good views of the water cascading through a beautiful gorge it has carved out. The edges may be unstable along the gorge, so keep a safe distance.

From small openings in the forest there are good views of Red Eagle, Mahtotopa, Little Chief and Citadel mountains. At 16.3 km the trail intersects the short path from Sun Road to a viewpoint where Baring Creek is funnelled through Sunrift Gorge--a deep, narrow fracture in the rock. Sun Road and the end of this hike are a short distance down the trail at point **G (16.4 km)**.

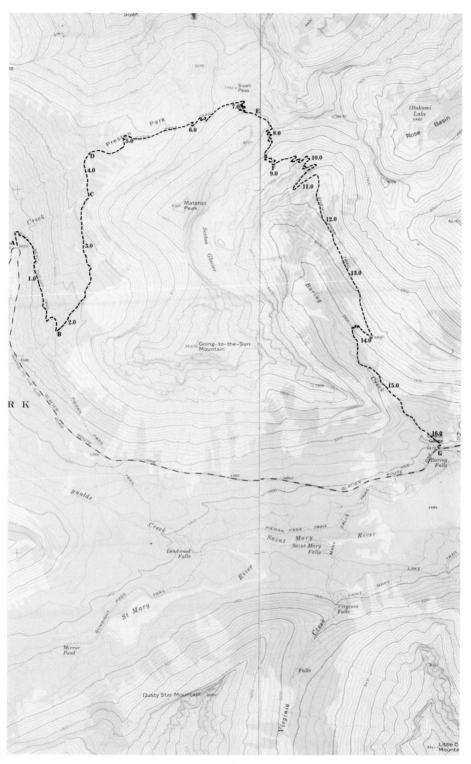

Cutthroat trout

Fisherman

Old mining machinery--Cracker Lake

Wildflowers on cliff

SNYDER LAKE

Summary: The first part of this hike is the same as the hikes to Mount Brown Lookout and Fish Lake. It follows the Gunsight Pass Trail from Sun Road near Lake McDonald Lodge, climbing along the north side of Snyder Creek to a junction with Mount Brown Lookout Trail. It then continues a short distance farther to another junction where it leaves Gunsight Pass Trail and takes Snyder Lake Trail to the left. It follows Snyder Lake Trail through an area of dense forest and shrubbery to Snyder Lake. This is an attractive lake situated in a small valley, partially surrounded by high slopes.

Length:
   One way - 7.1 km
   Round trip - 14.2 km
Dayhike or backpack
Season: Mid June
Vehicle shuttle: No
Elevation extremes: 975-1566 m
Topographic maps:
   Lake McDonald East
   Mount Cannon

The trailhead is on the east side of Sun Road across from a road exiting the parking area at Lake McDonald Lodge. The exit road and the trailhead are about 65 meters north of where Snyder Creek goes under Sun Road. The first part of this hike follows Gunsight Pass Trail which eventually goes on to Sperry Chalets.

The trail leaves Sun Road (A; 0.0) and passes the horse stables which are to the left of the trail about 80 meters from the start. It then passes to the right of a fenced treatment plant at 130 meters, and Snyder Creek is close to the trail on the right. The route continues to climb, passing through a very pretty forest of western red cedar. This is a lush area, dimly lit, blanketed with moss, ferns and wildflowers. There is usually some distance between the trail and the creek, but the roar of water can generally be heard, especially during the early part of the season when melting snows increase the run-off.

There is a junction at point B (2.8 km) where Mount Brown Lookout Trail goes left (see "Mount Brown Lookout"), but the trail described here continues ahead. There is another junction at point C (2.9 km). Gunsight Pass Trail continues ahead (see "Gunsight Pass" and "Fish Lake"), and the Snyder Lake Trail goes left. From here to the lake, the hike is generally uphill, although it is seldom steep. Vegetation is usually dense--huckleberries, meadowrue, arnicas, queencup bead-lilies, thimbleberries, bracken ferns (the list is almost endless). Cow-parsnip, a favorite food of bears, also grows along the trail. Western larches and thinleaf alders are common, and Engelmann spruce grows near the lake.

The last time we made this hike, several other hikers saw a black bear on the trail, but we saw only the tracks and droppings. There were also tracks of mountain goats. A number of the rocks in the trail had scats on them which we presumed to be territorial markers of mink, pine marten or weasel.

The trail is more or less parallel to Snyder Creek, but the dense vegetation permits only an occasional glimpse of the water below. The creek can usually be heard, however. The trail crosses a big rock slide on the side of Mount Brown. Pikas live here, and many of the rocks have a veneer of chartreuse-colored lichens.

The landscape opens up as the trail approaches the lake. It drops down to the shore at point D (7.1 km). Snyder Lake is situated 1566 meters above sea level and is usually a deep, dark green. A few small trout may be visible in the shallows and among the logs that float near the outlet. The falls at the far end come from Upper Snyder Lake which is not visible from here.

Part of Mount Brown can be seen from the shore. Little Matterhorn rises above Upper Snyder Lake, and Edwards Mountain is to the right of Snyder. Mountain goats can often be spotted on the cliffs of Edwards.

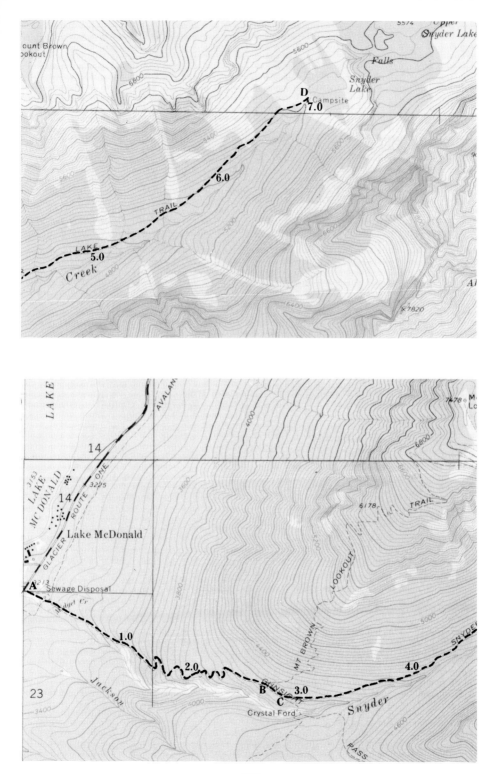

SWIFTCURRENT LOOKOUT

Summary: The trail begins near the Swiftcurrent Coffee Shop in Many Glacier. It climbs gradually, passing Fishercap, Redrock and Bullhead lakes, then climbs steeply from Bullhead Lake to Swiftcurrent Pass. The pass is near timberline. A short distance southwest of the pass, the hike described here follows a side trail that climbs above the meadows and subalpine firs to Swiftcurrent Lookout. The upper reaches of the climb are over a jumble of barren, angular rocks, the crevices of which are chinked with just enough soil to nurture miniature plants with miniature flowers. And the view from the top is one of the finest in the park.

Length:
   One way - 13.2 km
   Round trip - 26.4 km
Dayhike
Season: Early July
Vehicle shuttle: No
Elevation extremes: 1502-2571 m
Topographic maps:
   Many Glacier
   Ahern Pass

The hike starts at the northwest corner of the parking lot in front of Swiftcurrent Coffee Shop. (This lot is at the end of Many Glacier Road.) From the trailhead (A; 0.0) the route proceeds west for a little over 50 meters to a trail junction. This hike follows Swiftcurrent Pass Trail, which is the left fork.

At about 0.1 km a bridge spans Wilbur Creek. From here there are good views of Grinnell Point, Mount Wilbur and Mount Henkel, as well as Swiftcurrent Mountain high above to the west. From the bridge, the trail gradually climbs through an area of lodgepole pines. At 0.4 km a short side trail drops down on the left to Fishercap Lake.

Much of this first part of the hike is through an open landscape created by a fire which swept down from Swiftcurrent Pass in 1936. Shrubbery thrives in the open, sunny valley, interrupted occasionally by scattered stands of lodgepole pines and aspens which are struggling to begin reforestation in a particularly severe environment. You'll notice that the tops of many of the trees have been killed by freezing temperatures, heavy snows and driving winds.

The trail continues to a beautiful, rather shallow lake in a basin of red mudstone from which it takes its name, Redrock Lake. The trail swings around the head of the lake where there is a short side trail at point B (2.8 km) which goes to Redrock Falls. Here Swiftcurrent Creek plunges in a series of falls over the red mudstone into the lake (another of those watery places that look so tempting--but can turn out to be so treacherous--on a warm summer day).

At 4.3 km the trail passes an unnamed lake, then continues to Bullhead Lake at 5.1 km. The trail crosses a creek draining Windmaker Lake at point C (5.2 km). It then passes around the head of Bullhead Lake where there are a number of subalpine firs with dead tops. At point D (6.3 km) the trail passes a creek which comes down from Swiftcurrent Glacier. In general, the trail has been gradually uphill from the trailhead. Most of the route from near point D to Swiftcurrent Pass is very steep and arduous. There is a short breather just west of the pass, but it is quickly followed by another rugged climb to the lookout. Be in condition, and pace yourself.

Shrubs grow along the trail as it switchbacks uphill. Elderberry, thimbleberry, huckleberry and mountain ash are among the more common species. As the elevation increases and the exposure changes, grasses and other low-growing plants tend to replace the shrubs. Dead snags still stand, left in the wake of the 1936 Fire. The fire started on the Glacier Wall, crossed McDonald Creek and continued up past "the Loop" on Sun Road to Swiftcurrent Pass. From the vicinity of the pass, it swept down into the valley, reaching the area of Many Glacier in about forty-five minutes.

There are some nice views from the trail as it continues its climb--Bullhead

Lake, the un-named lake, Red Rock Lake, Windmaker Lake, Lake Sherburne and the Swiftcurrent Valley. There are also views of Swiftcurrent Glacier which is situated just below the Continental Divide. The trail occasionally diagonals along steep cliffs where there are some sheer drops.

At point **E (9.4 km)** the trail makes its last major switchback before reaching the pass. Subalpine firs grow in dense thickets, and the general area has distinct subalpine characteristics. Wildflowers such as beargrass, giant helleborine, moss campion, silky phacelia, red mountainheath, valerian and glacier-lilies grow on the open green turf along the trail. Columbian ground squirrels are common in the area, and patches of snow may persist until late in the season.

Recent studies have indicated that many subalpine and alpine plants can be severely damaged by off-trail hikers. The basic problem is that these plants have a very short growing and reproductive season and that this season is virtually identical to the period of heaviest park use. Experiments indicate that one person walking over a particular area just once a week during the season will reduce the overall plant growth by about nine percent. Additional tramplings (say up to fifty per week) can increase the reduction in plant cover by something like eighty-five percent. Keep in mind that these are general figures, but they **are** large. In addition to reducing the plant cover in these delicate areas, foot travel also results in possible long-term changes in the species composition of an area. Some plant species are less resilient than others.

One interesting plant which grows along the trail in the meadows near Swiftcurrent Pass is a species of dwarf willow. Like similar species which grow in the arctic regions, these plants are often only a few centimeters high and grow in the form of small mats. Like the other species of willows reported for the park (twenty or so), dwarf willows produce catkins and have a single bud scale.

Swiftcurrent Pass (elevation 2225 meters) is a broad saddle at point **F (10.9 km)**. The top of Swiftcurrent Lookout can be seen high above. There is a rock cairn located at the pass, and--in accordance with a European custom--there was a bell here to be rung by hikers. The bell was removed for a scrap drive during World War II. While the European custom is interesting, the more subtle sounds of wind and wildlife are just as enjoyable, if not more so. Subalpine firs grow at the pass, and it should be kept in mind that this is prime grizzly habitat. It is also a good place to see white-tailed ptarmigan.

From the pass, the trail drops down to a junction at point **G (11.0 km)**. From this junction, the Swiftcurrent Pass Trail continues ahead for 1.2 km to Granite Park Chalet. The trail described here diagonals back to the right/north from the junction and begins a stiff climb to the lookout atop Swiftcurrent Mountain. From the junction to the lookout, there is an elevation gain of 392 meters. Subalpine firs grow along the first switchbacks but soon drop behind.

There are large areas of relatively bare rock, and there is a talus-like layer over much of the upper part of the mountain. From a distance, the upper part of the mountain looks sterile, but this is very deceiving. Plant life is abundant, but much of it grows very close to the ground and often forms mats. Colorful lichens adorn many of the rocks, and the wildflowers...! To name a few, we saw saxifrage, five-leaved snow cinquefoil, cutleaf daisy, wild candytuft, skypilot and white dryad.

The trail continues to switchback and climb steeply, traversing small ledges and talus. The lookout, which is manned during the summer, is at point **H (13.2 km)** at an elevation of 2571 meters. Warning: There are some sheer dropoffs along the north side of the mountain, so don't approach the edge too closely.

The summit is worth a long pause to recuperate, explore and take in the magnificent view. Some of the mammals to look for include pikas, golden-mantled ground squirrels,

Columbian ground squirrels and mountain goats. The latter occasionally promenade around the catwalk of the lookout tower. Some of the birds which are occasionally seen here include bald eagles, golden eagles, white-tailed ptarmigans, gray-crowned rosy finches, prairie falcons and red-tailed hawks. On a sunny day, an amazing variety of insects can be found.

The list of landmarks visible from the summit is long, and the large topo of the park is a great aid in identifying them. We counted nine lakes, forty-eight major peaks and four glaciers. A real connoisseur of topography could probably come up with a lot more.

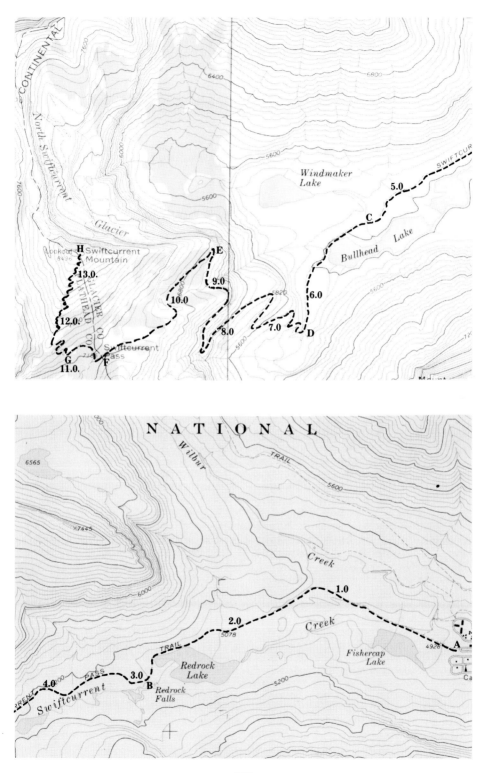

UPPER TWO MEDICINE LAKE

Summary: From the trailhead near Two Medicine Campground, this trail first parallels the north shore of Two Medicine Lake, then continues west. It gradually climbs, passing the short spur trail to Twin Falls. It then continues to climb to Upper Two Medicine Lake, a sizeable body of water surrounded by pine-fir forest, willows and scree and an august assembly of peaks.

Length:
  One way - 7.3 km
  Round trip - 14.6 km
Dayhike or overnight
Season: Mid June
Vehicle shuttle: No
Elevation extremes: 1574-1676 m
Topographic maps:
  Squaw Mountain
  Mount Rockwell

If you plan to ride the boat back up Two Medicine Lake, be sure to check the schedule before you start this hike.

From Two Medicine Campground, the trailhead is reached by crossing the bridge below the outlet of Pray Lake. (This is a small lake just to the west of the campground, and the bridge is easy to spot.) The distance from the road to the trailhead across the bridge is 137 meters. Here there is a "T" in the trail. Pitamakin Pass Trail goes to the right (see "Oldman Lake"); the hike to Upper Two Medicine Lake starts (A; 0.0) by going left on Dawson Pass Trail.

The fairly level first part of the trail soon passes Pray Lake. Willow thickets crowd its margins and are a habitat favored by the yellow warbler. These small birds appear to be entirely yellow from a distance.

This hike provides an excellent opportunity to observe many species of wildflowers. Some of the ones we identified along the trail one morning included thimbleberry, twinflower, lupine, yarrow, stonecrop, yellow penstemon, forget-me-not, cow-parsnip, thistle, mountain ash, alum-root, mariposa lily, Indian-paintbrush, false Solomon's seal and many more. Botany isn't our field, yet we found that with very little effort we were able to identify dozens of species of Glacier's wildflowers by using a combination of three or four popular wildflower guides.

The trail passes through stands of firs and other trees interspersed with some relatively open areas. The route is about 25-50 meters above Two Medicine Lake and about 50-250 meters from the shoreline. There is a disheveled collection of trees in an avalanche chute at 1.3 km. These chutes can often be spotted across Glacier's valleys. They are characterized by an open, vertical path bordered by forest on both sides. Avalanches are a common phenomenon in the high-country during the winter and spring. They tend to occur at the same places year after year. Sometimes wild animals are trapped under them and kept frozen until the spring thaw. Grizzlies check these areas in the spring for victims such as mountain goats. There have been human fatalities in the park when climbers were buried beneath avalanches.

Paradise Point is on the opposite side of the lake at about 1.4 km. Farther on, a small log bridge crosses a creek at point B (3.4 km). Black cottonwoods, thinleaf alders and Rocky Mountain maples grow along its edges. Here the trail has begun to pull away from the lake but is not far from the western end.

Dawson Pass Trail follows the right-hand fork at a junction at point C (4.8 km), passing near No Name Lake before climbing to Dawson Pass. The route to Upper Two Medicine Lake follows the lefthand fork from the junction at point C. There is another junction at point D (a little over 5.0 km). From here there is a trail heading back toward Two Medicine Lake. It goes to Pray Shelter and the boat dock, and the South Shore Trail branches off from it near the lake.

From the junction at point D, the trail described here follows the right-hand fork. It crosses a fair-sized tributary of Two Medicine Creek at point E (5.2 km). Pumpelly Pillar is visible to the west from here. At point **F** (5.3 km) there is yet another junction where a short side trail goes right/northwest to Twin Falls.

The side trip to the falls is worthwhile. In fact, many people take the boat trip up the lake just to see the beautiful pair of cascading falls. No falls or swift stream in Glacier would be complete without one or two of the small gray birds known as "dippers" or water ouzels. Look for them here, especially around the pool at the base of the left falls. They dip up and down when perched on rocks just above the water's surface, and they often dive completely under water as they pursue food in the form of insects such as caddisflies, mayflies and stoneflies. They construct large nests of mosses, often tucked up on ledges behind waterfalls. If you do not see any dippers when you first arrive at the falls, be patient--one will appear more often than not. When they fly, they skim closely above the running water, making turns wherever the stream does. We watched a young bird working tentatively in the quieter part of the pool while an older bird repeatedly flew into the falls, only to pop up like a cork in the pool below.

From the junction at point F, the trail continues toward Upper Two Medicine Lake. Spruce-fir forest alternates with partially open areas where shrubs such as menziesia, pink meadowsweet, elderberry and mountain ash are abundant. Bears often feed in areas such as these, and black bears or grizzlies could be encountered anywhere in the park. Anyone hiking in the bears' domain should be alert and cautious. We saw no grizzlies while researching the trails for this book, although we've seen them other years. In fact, the longer we went without seeing one, the more we expected to and the more alert we became. We know one individual who was treed by a grizzly along this particular trail.

At the 6.8-km point, the trail passes to the right/north of a shallow, unnamed lake (elevation 5410 on the topo). The grade levels out as the trail nears its destination. The edge of Upper Two Medicine Lake is at point

G (7.3 km). The slopes of Rising Bull Ridge are above the south shore; those of Mount Helen and Pumpelly Pillar rise above the north shore, and Lone Walker looms over the far end. There are some brook trout in the lake, but they tend to be rather small. California gulls occasionally wheel over the lake, sometimes dipping down to snatch up a fish.

If you wish to return on the boat, hike back the way you came until you reach point D, then turn right and proceed 1.2 km to Pray Shelter and the boat dock at Two Medicine Lake.

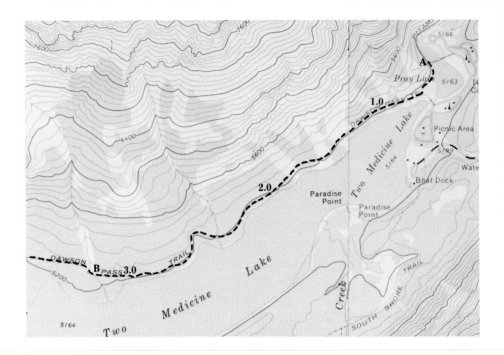

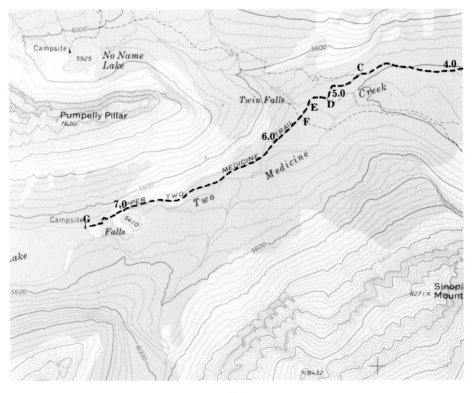

WATERTON LAKE

Summary: This hike involves taking a boat from the head of Waterton Lake in Waterton Lakes National Park down to Glacier National Park. A trail then returns to the Canadian park by going north along the west side of the lake, crossing the International Boundary enroute. Virtually all of the hike is through forest which affords only occasional views of the lake.

Length:
   One way - 13.9 km
Dayhike
Season: Mid June
Vehicle shuttle: No
Elevation extremes: 1279-1370 m
Topographic map:
   Porcupine Ridge

When planning this trip, be sure to check current regulations regarding entry into Canada. There may also be some regulations to comply with when re-entering Canada on foot.

The hike described here incorporates a boat ride from Waterton Townsite, Canada, down the length of Waterton Lake to Goat Haunt in Glacier National Park in the United States. The M.V. "International" has been plying these waters since 1927, and boat schedules are available at Emerald Bay in Waterton Townsite. Plan your departure to allow plenty of time for the hike back. A fare is charged for the boat ride; however, there is usually a good little spiel about the lake and the landmarks during the ride down to Goat Haunt.

There is a visitor complex at Goat Haunt where the boat docks. The trailhead is reached by hiking around the foot of the lake to a shelter and small ranger station about 400 meters from the dock. The trailhead (A; 0.0) is about 40 meters beyond the ranger station. The left fork is the Waterton Valley Trail which heads south from here, passes the Kootenai Lakes and joins the Stoney Indian Pass Trail. The righthand fork is Waterton Lake Trail, and all distances are measured from this point.

The trail soon leaves a paved walk and is shaded by Engelmann spruce, lodgepole pine and an occasional black cottonwood or quaking asken. At 0.5 km there is a trail going to the right to a horse ford across the Waterton River.

At point **B (0.9 km)** there is a trail junction. A relatively short trail goes 0.7 km from here to Rainbow Falls on the Waterton River. This is a popular destination for many who take the boat down the lake and wish to make a short hike. The trail destined for Waterton Townsite heads toward the river and crosses it at point **C** (a little over 0.9 km) via a suspension bridge. Just after crossing the river, an old trail goes left a short distance to Olson Falls, but the main trail goes right. Many of the trails around the south end of the lake have been changed since the topographic map was produced in 1968, and the trail alignments which we have shown should be considered approximate.

At point **D (1.1 km)** a side trail goes to the right, and the main trail continues ahead. It climbs several switchbacks to yet another junction at point **E (1.5 km)**. Boulder Pass Trail goes left/west from here; Waterton Lake Trail goes right/east. It drops gradually down to a junction at point **F (1.8 km)** where the horse ford trail comes in on the right. Shrubs such as Rocky Mountain maple and thimbleberry are common here. Thimbleberries have an interesting flavor, although most people do not like them quite as well as ripe huckleberries or wild strawberries.

The trail now heads north, passing through forest that varies from lodgepole pine to spruce or fir, depending on the locality. It more or less parallels the lake shore, but there are not many places where the lake can be seen from the trail. Boreal toads are sometimes found on this trail, and the loud chattering of red squirrels can often be heard. Shrubs are plentiful and may crowd the trail in places. Trail crews normally work most of Glacier's trails each year, cutting those shrubs which extend over the trail, brushing and doing major work such as building bridges. The first of a number of western paper birches grows along the trail at the 4-km point. Campbell Mountain can be seen off to the left at about 4.2 km.

One of the few viewpoints along the trail is at 5.4 km where the trail skirts a rocky beach. There is a trail junction at point **G (6.3 km)** where there is another horse ford. Since Boundary Creek carries a considerable amount of water, it is necessary for hikers to go to the left/west here, through the forest and more or less parallel to the creek. At point **H (6.6 km)** there is another junction. From here the North Boundary trail takes off straight ahead/west while the Waterton Lake trail goes right and crosses Boundary Creek via a wooden bridge at point **I (6.7 km)**. Here the water shoots through a narrows and over a small falls, and a larger falls can be seen upstream. Lodgepole pines grow in the vicinity.

The trail soon pulls away from the creek, and at point **J (6.9 km)** it merges with the horse ford trail which diagonals in from the right. The route continues north to the International Boundary at point **K (7.2 km)** where an eight-meter swath has been cut through the forest to define the boundary line. There are two monuments here, also a boat dock on the U.S. side and a warden's cabin on the Canadian side.

From the boundary, the trail continues north. **(No map is shown for this last section.)** In general, the trail on the Canadian side has a few more ups and downs, but it otherwise continues through forest. There is a small, rocky beach at 8.5 km. Lodgepoles form dense stands in several places, and there are also some nice stands of quaking aspens (so named because their leaf stems are flattened, causing the leaves to flutter in the slightest breeze). There are occasional views of parts of Waterton Lake from the trail. At the 11-km point, the Prince of Wales Hotel can be seen for the first time from the trail. It was constructed in 1926-1927 by the Great Northern Railroad, and its architectural style is impressive, to say the least. At the top of a long hill at 12.1 km, there is a trail junction. The trail to Bertha Lake goes left, and the trail to Waterton Townsite goes right.

At 12.5 km a short side trail goes to a viewpoint on the right. Several peaks are visible to the east of the lake, and Mount Cleveland is visible back in Glacier. The latter is Glacier Park's highest point (3190 meters). Not far beyond the viewpoint, Waterton Townsite can be seen with Mount Crandell above it. At one area along the trail and not far from the townsite, lodgepole pines lie scattered about on the ground, the result of unusually heavy winds. The townsite itself, which is built on an alluvial fan of Cameron Creek, is often battered by strong prevailing winds.

The trail ends at the edge of Waterton Townsite at 13.9 km. It is only a short hike from here to a main road west of the campground, and the center of town can be reached by following that road either way. The townsite has a number of facilities and makes a good place to relax after a long hike.

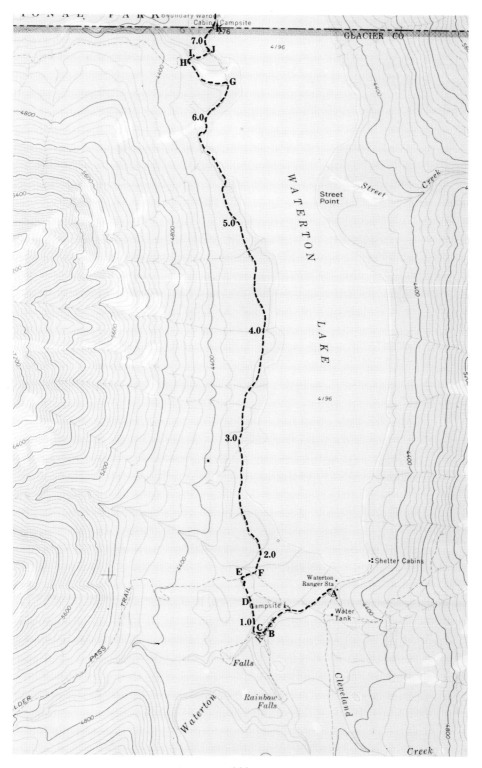